All Our Yesterdays

Cross Stitch Collection

33 CHARMING DESIGNS FROM BYGONE DAYS

David and Charles

A DAVID & CHARLES BOOK
Copyright © David & Charles Limited 2007

David & Charles is an F+W Publications Inc. company
4700 East Galbraith Road
Cincinnati, OH 45236

First published in the UK in 2007

Layout and photography copyright © David & Charles 2007
Text and charted designs copyright © DMC Creative World Ltd 2007
Illustrations copyright © Faye Whittaker 2007

The publisher would like to thank Lin Clements for her evocative text contributions
and, of DMC Creative World, Cara Ackerman for her technical expertise and
Becky Jackson for chart co-ordination

A catalogue record for this book is available from the British Library.

ISBN-13: 978-0-7153-2471-4 hardback
ISBN-10: 0-7153-2471-3 hardback

ISBN-13: 978-0-7153-2472-1 paperback
ISBN-10: 0-7153-2472-1 paperback

Printed in China by SNP Leefung Pte Ltd
for David & Charles
Brunel House   Newton Abbot   Devon

Executive Editor Cheryl Brown
Desk Editor Bethany Dymond
Project Editor and Chart Preparation Lin Clements
Senior Designer Charly Bailey
Designer Eleanor Stafford
Styled Photography Kim Sayer
Photography Karl Adamson
Production Controller Ros Napper

Visit our website at www.davidandcharles.co.uk

David & Charles books are available from all good bookshops; alternatively you can contact our
Orderline on 0870 9908222 or write to us at FREEPOST EX2 110, D&C Direct, Newton Abbot,
TQ12 4ZZ (no stamp required UK only); US customers call 800-289-0963 and Canadian customers
call 800-840-5220.

CONTENTS

ALL OUR YESTERDAYS...

*I*n a celebration of the enchanting and evocative paintings of Faye Whittaker, *All Our Yesterdays Cross Stitch Collection* invites you on a trip down memory lane, to that halcyon period around the turn of the 20th century – a time of pleasure in simple things, of family holidays and children's games.

The cross stitch designs are rich with images of these bygone days, scenes filled with joie de vivre that remind us of the innocent pleasures of childhood – holidays by the sea, half-forgotten playground games, golden trips to the countryside and some of the special occasions that make the past a place of treasured memories.

Faye Whittaker, the Artist

Faye Whittaker was born in the beautiful Edwardian town of Southport in the north of England, famous for its sandy beach, donkeys, parasols and colourful beach huts.

Graduating from college with distinctions, Faye began a colourful period of travel to broaden her artistic palette. Arriving in San Francisco in California, she worked as a magazine illustrator during the week, while her weekends were spent painting for the tourists at Fisherman's Wharf. This happy time came to an end when her visa expired but, undeterred, Faye headed for the south of France, where she lived and worked as a street artist for the next five years. It was here that she studied the effects of sunlight and reflections and began to concentrate on painting what was to become a distinctive style – impressionist-style children at the water's edge, usually viewed from behind.

" I soon began to realize that my paintings appealed to most people as they could visualize their own little ones being the characters in the paintings. "

" It was my early memories of Southport and other seaside towns nearby that first inspired me as an artist and from an early age I was rarely seen without a sketch pad in my hand. "

Returning to England with a wealth of valuable experience Faye settled in the cosmopolitan town of Brighton in the south coast. Here she combined her love of children and the seaside, and created the enchanting watercolour paintings that were to become the 'All Our Yesterdays' collection. She made a name for herself with these attractive, nostalgic works, selling them through art galleries she had established and craft shows nationwide. It was at one of these shows that DMC, Britain's largest cross stitch company, discovered Faye and quickly recognized the instant 'Ahhhh' appeal in her work.

DMC and All Our Yesterdays

DMC saw that Faye's delightful paintings could attract a whole world of new admirers if they were interpreted as cross stitch embroideries. Faye agreed and licensed the All Our Yesterdays collection to DMC and was soon their best-selling designer, her creations eagerly welcomed by stitchers all over Europe.

It was an exciting time for Faye and her work gained a fresh and very personal source of inspiration with the birth of her daughter, Jessica. Faye's creativity, and baby Jessica, flourished and Faye became one of the most sought-after water colourists in Britain.

" I had never seen my work stitched before – the paintings just came to life."

" My beautiful baby Jessica was, and still is, the main inspiration of my life. She is my perfect model and appears in many of my works. My first piece called 'Raggetty Anne' was painted when my daughter Jessica was two, clutching a dolly my mother had made for her, and it remains my all-time favourite!"

There is no doubt that people love Faye's designs and she has been honoured with the unprecedented achievement of being named Designer of the Year for three years in a row, voted by readers of the top cross stitch magazines. The All Our Yesterdays collection now consists of over 100 evocative designs, available as originals, prints and, of course, cross stitch. The designs can be found on many products worldwide, products as diverse as fine bone china mugs, thimbles and sun-catchers, and the future of the collection looks assured as Faye celebrates ten years with DMC.

You too can enter the atmospheric world of Faye Whittaker and bring back a little of the magic of yesteryear with this collection of utterly beguiling designs.

I hope you enjoy stitching these scenes as much as I enjoyed painting them!
Bye for now
Faye

Visit the world of Faye Whittaker at
www.fayewhittakerarts.com

INTO THE BLUE

" Blue skies

Smiling at me,

Nothing but blue skies do I see. "

(Irving Berlin, 1927)

There are some scenes from our past that stay in the mind, the memory of the event just waiting to be recalled by a sound, a scent or a touch. Such scenes may be historical events that thousands share or just simple but evocative pictures from our childhood. This chapter features two very different scenes – one under the azure blue sky of day time and one amid the dark sapphire of night time.

Transfixed, children watch a neck-and-neck hot-air balloon race, holding their breath as the huge balloons skim the water and begin to rise. On the peaceful beach they hear the roar of the burner and the laughter of the passengers and wish they too were rising into the blue.

Later in the day, excited children wait impatiently for the sun to sink below the horizon, for the night sky to deepen and the fireworks begin! It is their first experience of the sight and one they will never forget – the noise and excitement, the glittering flashes of explosive colour lighting up the night and the pungent smell of drifting smoke; that distinctive fireworks smell that will forever recall memories of the event.

Balloon Race

Oh, for the time to rise above the hustle and bustle, to drift where the wind takes you. Hot-air balloons belong to the past and this picture takes us effortlessly back in time to a more graceful age. A companion night-time scene appears on page 9.

Balloon Race

This colourful design paints an evocative picture of serene transport from a bygone age but children today would be just as fascinated by the sight of two hot-air balloons setting off on an exciting race.

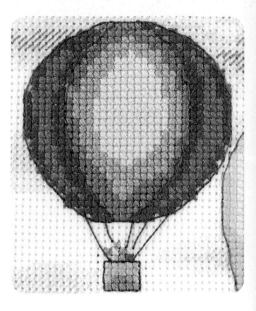

BALLOON RACE (PAGE 7)

Fabric
16-count ivory Aida (DMC DC88 712), 40.5 × 33cm (16 × 13in)

Threads
DMC stranded cotton (floss) as listed in the key – 1 skein of each colour and 2 skeins of 334, 677, 746, 775 and 3325

Stitch Count
176h × 119w

Design Size
28 × 19cm (11 × 7½in)

Stitches
Whole cross stitch, half cross stitch, backstitch

Stitch the Scene. . .
Prepare your fabric for work and mark the centre point (see page 98). Follow the chart on pages 12–13 and work over one block of Aida, using two strands of stranded cotton for cross stitches. Work the half cross stitches with one or two strands, as indicated in the chart key. Work backstitches with one strand. The strings of the balloons can be long straight stitches over a number of Aida squares. When all stitching is complete, mount and frame your picture.

Fireworks Night

The sheer spectacle of a fireworks display is hard to beat and just the thing to mark an important celebration, such as the turn of a century. This atmospheric design is given extra sparkle by the use of Light Effects threads.

FIREWORKS NIGHT

Fabric
16-count ivory Aida (DMC DC88 712), 40.5 × 33cm (16 × 13in)

Threads
DMC stranded cotton (floss) as listed in the key – 1 skein of each colour and 3 skeins of 311; DMC Light Effects as listed in the key

Stitch Count
168h × 131w

Design Size
27 × 21cm (10½ × 8¼in)

Stitches
Whole cross stitch, three-quarter cross stitch, half cross stitch, backstitch

Stitch the Scene. . .
Prepare your fabric for work and mark the centre point (see page 98). Follow the chart on pages 14–15 and work over one block of Aida, using two strands of stranded cotton for full and half cross stitches. Use two strands for Light Effects cross stitches (see page 99 for advice). Work backstitches with one strand. When all stitching is complete, mount and frame your picture.

Up, Up and Away

This charming design makes a perfect card – perhaps a birthday card, with the recipient's name stitched above the design using one of the backstitch alphabets on page 97, or a bon voyage card for someone going on a journey.

UP, UP AND AWAY

Fabric
16-count ivory Aida (DMC DC88 712), 18 × 18cm (7 × 7in)

Threads
DMC stranded cotton (floss) as listed in the key – 1 skein of each colour

Stitch Count
68h × 59w

Design Size
10.8 × 9.4cm (4¼ × 3¾in)

Stitches
Whole cross stitch, half cross stitch, backstitch

Stitch the Scene. . .
Prepare your fabric for work and mark the centre point (see page 98). Follow the chart opposite and work over one block of Aida, using two strands of stranded cotton for full and half cross stitches. Work backstitches with one strand. When all stitching is complete, mount into a card – see page 101.

Firework Magic

Capture the magic of a brilliant firework against a night sky in a lovely greetings card – an ideal design to experiment with Light Effects metallic threads.

FIREWORK MAGIC

Fabric
16-count ivory Aida (DMC DC88 712), 20.3 × 20.3cm (8 × 8in)

Threads
DMC stranded cotton (floss) and Light Effects as listed in the key – 1 skein of each colour

Stitch Count
77h × 53w

Design Size
12.3 × 8.4cm (4¾ × 3¼in)

Stitches
Whole cross stitch, half cross stitch, backstitch

Stitch the Scene. . .
Prepare your fabric for work and mark the centre point (see page 98). Follow the chart opposite and work over one block of Aida, using two strands of stranded cotton for full and half cross stitches. Use two strands for Light Effects cross stitches (see page 99 for advice). Work backstitches with one strand. When all stitching is complete, mount into a card – see page 101.

Up, Up and Away

DMC stranded cotton

Full cross stitch (2 strands)

—	223	×	729	+	3042
	224	O	746	↑	3325
•	312		840		3721
V	318	I	898		3774
	334	/	950	•	blanc
	677		3041		

Half cross stitch (2 strands)

	3325
	3347
\	3348

Backstitch (1 strand)

— 413

Firework Magic

DMC stranded cotton

Full cross stitch (2 strands)

U	304		666	+	3042
	310		677	↑	3325
•	312	×	729	/	3705
	334	O	746		3774
	413		3041	•	blanc

Half cross stitch

(2 strands)

	312
	3347
\	3348

DMC Light Effects

Full cross stitch (2 strands)

	E703
	E718
	E3849

Backstitch (1 strand)

— 413

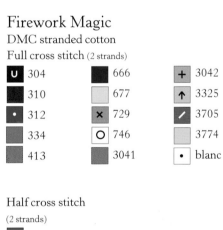

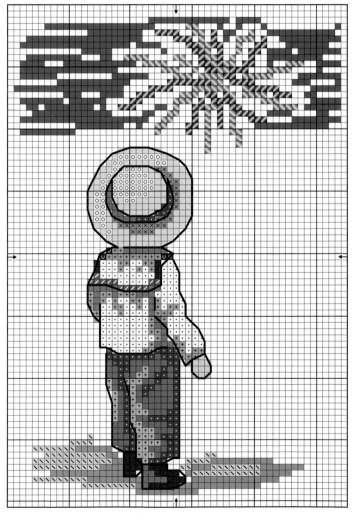

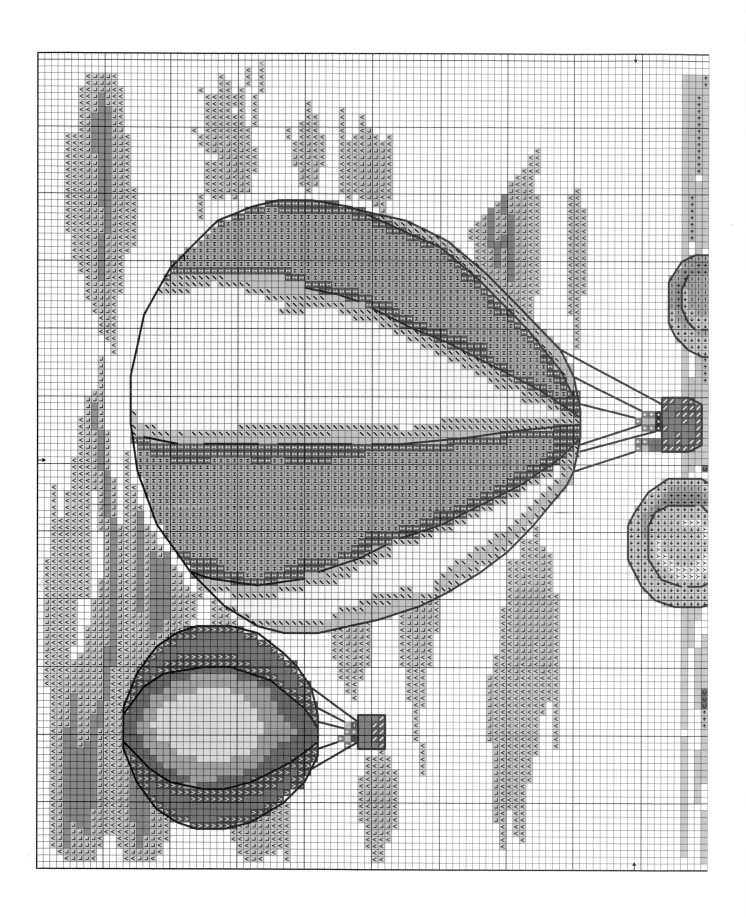

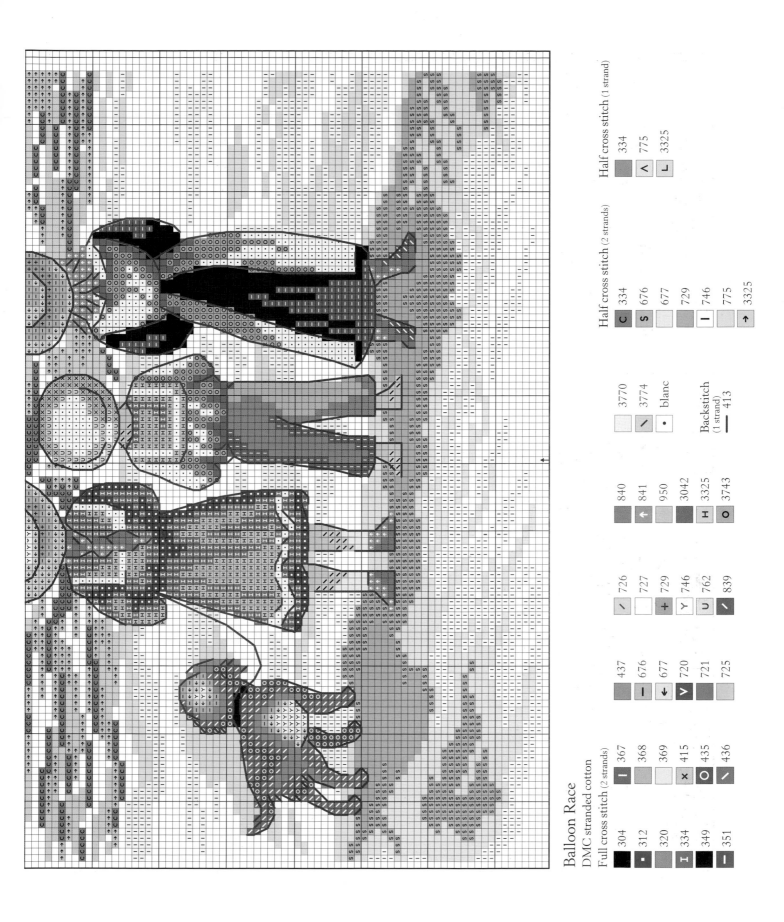

Balloon Race

DMC stranded cotton

Full cross stitch (2 strands)

304		437	/	726	/	840		3770	
312	·	676	I	727		841	←	3774	/
320		677	↓	729	+	950		blanc	·
334	I	720	Y	746	Y	3042			
349	O	721	U	762	U	3325	H		
351	—	725	/	839	/	3743	O		

Half cross stitch (2 strands)

334	C
676	S
677	
729	I
746	
775	
3325	↑

Half cross stitch (1 strand)

334	
775	∧
3325	L

Backstitch (1 strand)

— 413

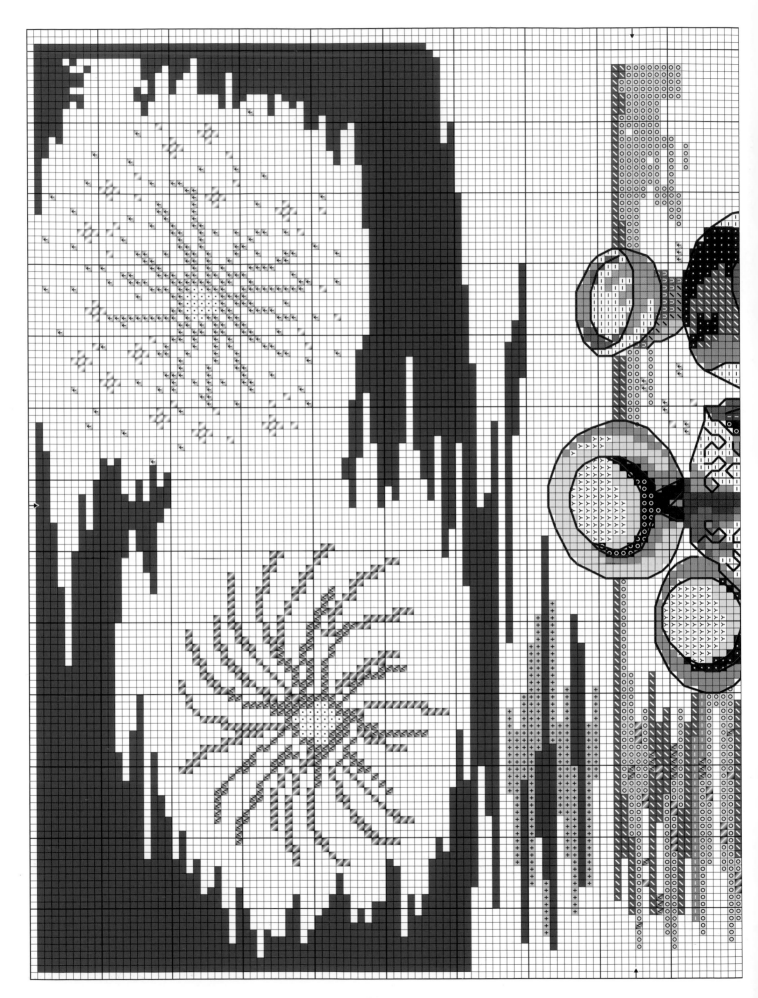

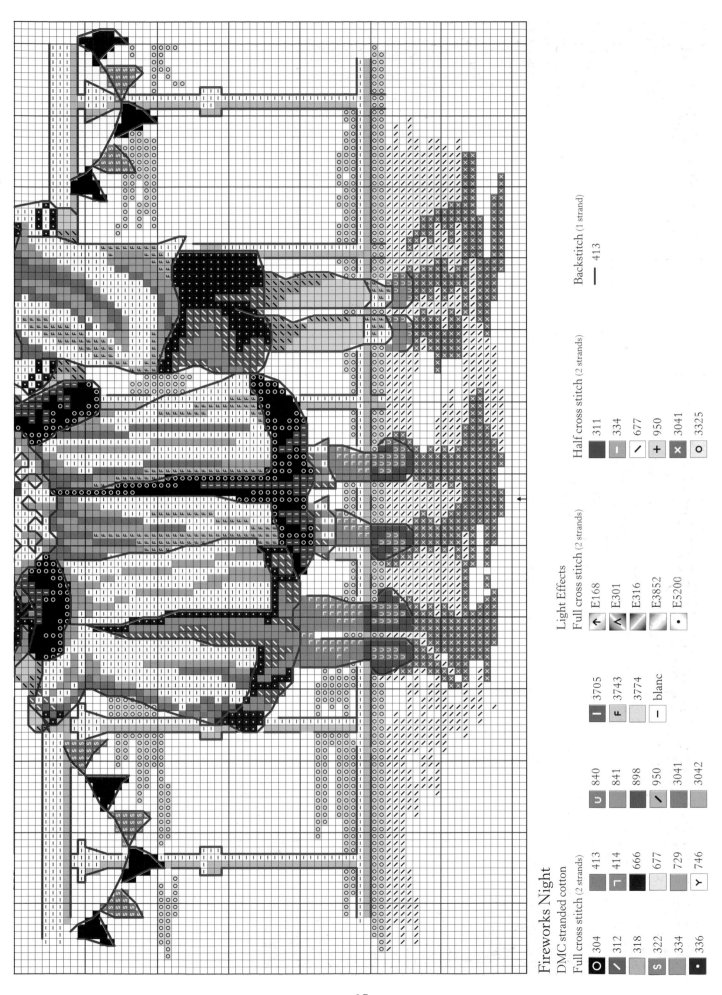

Fireworks Night

DMC stranded cotton

Full cross stitch (2 strands)

O	304
/	312
	318
S	322
	334
•	336

U	840
	841
	898
/	950
	3041
	3042

I	3705
F	3743
	3774
—	blanc

L	414
	413
	666
	677
	729
Y	746

Light Effects

Full cross stitch (2 strands)

←	E168
<	E301
/	E316
	E3852
•	E5200

Half cross stitch (2 strands)

	311
I	334
/	677
+	950
×	3041
O	3325

Backstitch (1 strand)

— 413

BOAT RACE

Oh I do like to be beside the seaside,

Oh I do like to be beside the sea.

I do like to stroll along the prom, prom, prom,

Where the brass bands play, tiddly-om-pom-pom.

(Music hall song by John Glover-Kind, 1907)

By 1900 the seaside was all the rage, with its donkeys, piers, boarding houses and landladies. The railways were bringing increasing hordes of people to the coast, particularly at weekends, but 'genteel' visitors could still find peaceful resorts and activities suitable for the family. These middle and upper

class visitors dressed only slightly less formally than at home. Skirts were still full and voluminous, but without the train. Large straw hats, often with ribbon streamers and gauze veils, were important – no 'lady' appeared bareheaded and they also protected her from an unfashionable sun tan. Young men were dressed with a nautical flavour, with shiny straw boaters, striped blazers and white flannels.

Well-to-do visitors took part in quiet, dignified activities, such as bowls, archery and croquet. The highlight of the day was the afternoon promenade, and piers allowed people to stroll out to sea without getting wet or undressing. There, they could watch acrobats, listen to a brass band or wave to a flotilla of yachts, sails billowing as they raced for the finishing buoy.

Blow Wind, Blow

In days gone by, there was always something going on at the seaside – an exciting yacht race, a visiting ocean liner or musicians performing on the newly built pier.

Blow Wind, Blow

An exciting yacht race has this charming group of spectators cheering. If you wish to bring additional texture to the design, work the cross stitch flowers in the lady's hat in French knots or replace the red cross stitches there with matching seed beads. See page 30 for working French knots.

 Remember when. . .?

Decades ago any seaside town worth its salt had a pier, not just a wooden landing stage but an ambitious construction of wrought iron, complete with bandstand pavilion and filled with varied entertainments.

BLOW WIND, BLOW (PAGE 17)

Fabric
16-count ivory Aida (DMC DC88 712), 48 × 40cm (19 × 16in)

Threads
DMC stranded cotton (floss) as listed in the key – 1 skein of each colour; 2 skeins of 312, 3042, 3325 and blanc and 3 skeins of 334

Stitch Count
214h × 169w

Design Size
34 × 26.8cm (13½ × 10½in)

Stitches
Whole cross stitch, half cross stitch, backstitch

Stitch the Scene. . .
Prepare your fabric for work and mark the centre point (see page 98). Follow the chart on pages 20–23 and work over one block of Aida, using two strands of stranded cotton for full and half cross stitches. Work backstitches with one strand. When all stitching is complete, mount and frame your picture.

Watching the Boats

Taking the dog for a walk at the seaside was an exciting prospect – always something to see. Perhaps later, if the children had been good, they would be taken to the pier to watch a Punch and Judy show.

WATCHING THE BOATS

Fabric
16-count ivory Aida (DMC DC88 712), 38 × 33cm (15 × 13in)

Threads
DMC stranded cotton (floss) as listed in the key – 1 skein of each colour and 2 skeins of 677, 3325 and blanc

Stitch Count
160h × 128w

Design Size
25.5 × 20.3cm (10 × 8in)

Stitches
Whole cross stitch, three-quarter cross stitch, half cross stitch, backstitch

Stitch the Scene. . .
Prepare your fabric for work and mark the centre point (see page 98). Follow the chart on pages 24–25 and work over one block of Aida, using two strands of stranded cotton for full and half cross stitches. Work backstitches with one strand. When all stitching is complete, mount and frame your picture.

USE THE SCENE. . .

The Watching the Boats scene could be stitched as a decoration on a photo album – perfect for holiday memories and snapshots. Back the stitching with iron-on interfacing (see page 100), glue it to the front of the album and then frame the patch with jaunty red rickrack braid, glued around the edge neatly.

Blow Wind, Blow

DMC stranded cotton

Full cross stitch (2 strands)

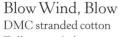

◤ 304	○ 318	◉ 347	676	✕ 729	840	◥ 950	❙ 3325	3774
• 310	334	436	╱ 677	746	869	✚ 3041	3347	• blanc
◢ 312	╱ 336	666	F 680	S 839	❙ 898	V 3042	− 3705	

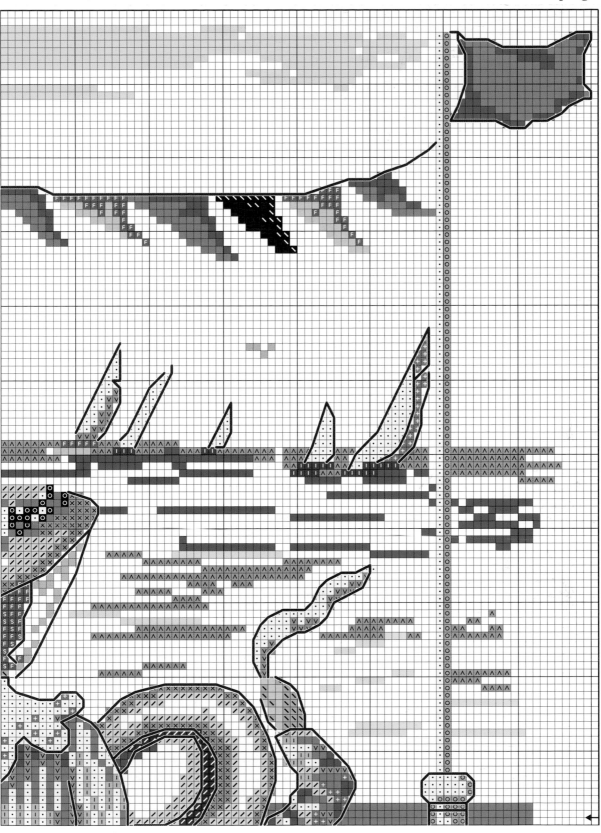

Half cross stitch (2 strands)

	318		677		3042
∧	334		3041		3325

Backstitch (1 strand)

— 413

Bottom left

Blow Wind, Blow

DMC stranded cotton

Full cross stitch (2 strands)

◥ 304	◉ 347	676	✕ 729	840	◥ 950	I 3325	3774
• 310	334	436	╱ 677	746	+ 3041	3347	• blanc
312	╱ 336	666	F 680	S 839	I 898	V 3042	− 3705
	◯ 318				869		

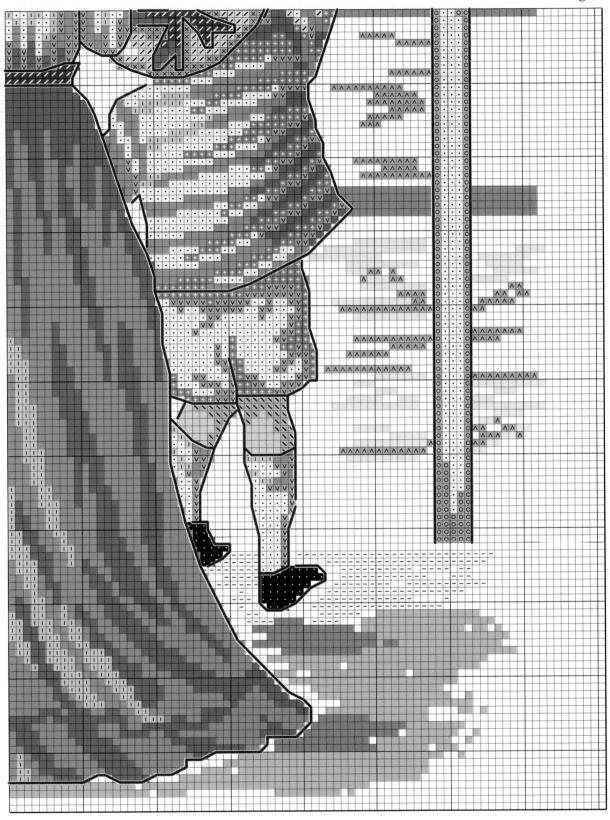

Half cross stitch (2 strands)

	318	—	677		3042
∧	334		3041		3325

Backstitch (1 strand)

— 413

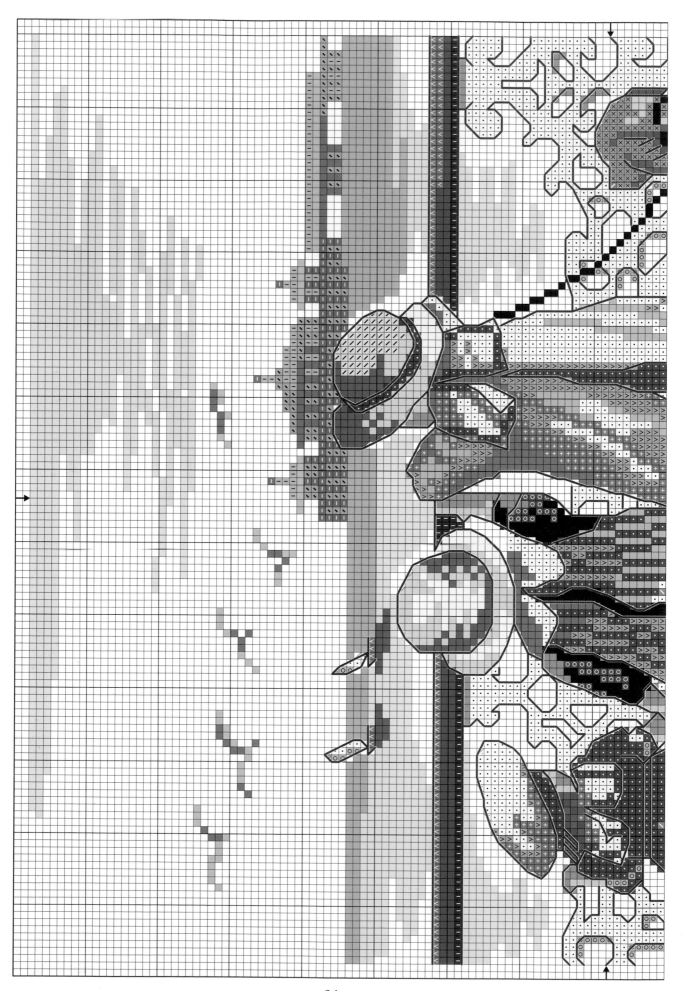

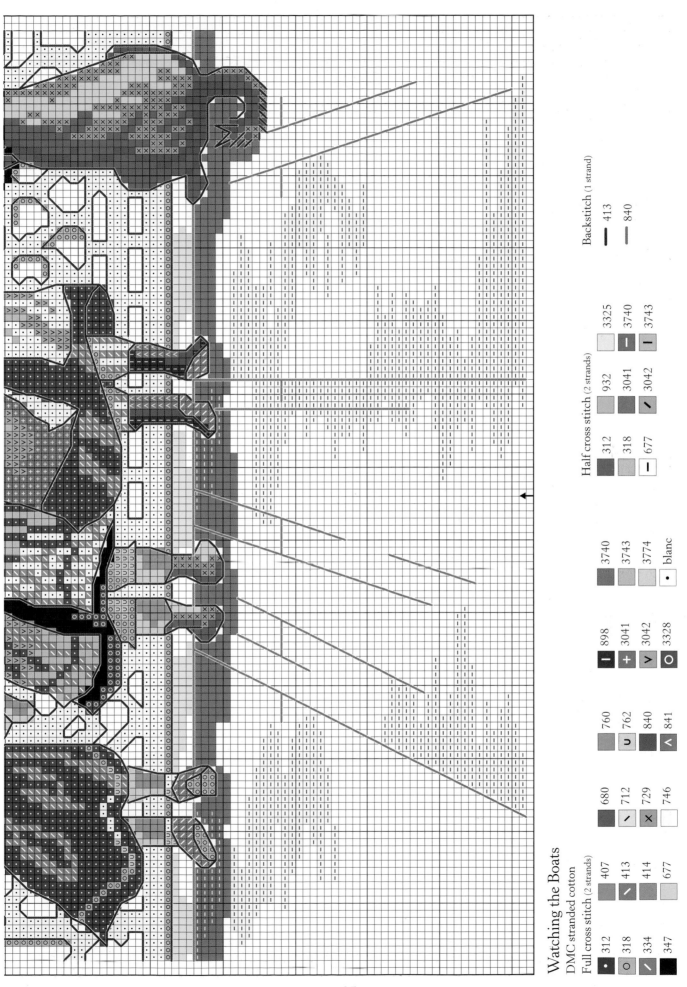

Watching the Boats

DMC stranded cotton

Full cross stitch (2 strands)

• 312	▨ 680	▨ 760	▨ 3740
○ 318	╱ 712	∪ 762	▨ 3743
╱ 334	✕ 729	▨ 840	▨ 3774
▨ 347	746	∨ 841	• blanc
	▬ 407	▬ 898	▨ 3325
	╱ 413	+ 3041	▬ 3740
	✕ 414	∨ 3042	▬ 3743
	677	○ 3328	

Half cross stitch (2 strands)

▨ 312	▨ 932		
▨ 318	▨ 3041		
─ 677	╲ 3042		

Backstitch (1 strand)

— 413
— 840

COUNTRYSIDE CHARMS

"A swarm of bees in May is worth a load of hay;
A swarm of bees in June is worth a silver spoon.
A swarm of bees in July isn't worth a fly."

(Traditional country lore)

To many of us, yesterday is a place as much as a time – a place where material things were scarce but where joy in simple pleasures was abundant. The countryside of yesterday was such a place, filled with subtle charms, where wildflowers were plentiful – not just poppies but primroses, bluebells, campions, cranesbills, foxgloves and ox-eye daisies. Come mid summer, come swallow time, there were yellowing head-high fields of wheat to roam in, rustling with warm breezes. A perfect afternoon saw children released from chores, picking wildflowers and watching the white breasts of swallows gleam as they performed their boomerang-like flights.

This rural idyll was a place where the land was still ploughed by steady horses, where a whole village worked in the wheat fields – for the reaping, the binding, the stacking of sheaves, the building of ricks. Even the youngest child helped with the gleaning, that gathering up of every last, precious stalk. Then the stubble would be visited by thousands of birds finding escaped grains and homeless insects – first a brown crowd of young sparrows issuing from nests in the barns, then linnets, greenfinches, buntings and greedy wood pigeons.

In the Poppy Meadow

Yesterday's childhood was a place filled with innocent pleasures – running hand in hand with a friend through a blazing scarlet carpet of poppies in the July meadow.

In the Poppy Meadow

This idyllic scene epitomizes all that is memorable about the charms of the countryside – sunshine, flowers, freedom and joy. The design would also look lovely made up into a cushion, perhaps with a floral fabric border.

IN THE POPPY MEADOW (PAGE 27)

Fabric
16-count ivory Aida (DMC DC88 712), 33 x 35.5cm (13 x 14in)

Threads
DMC stranded cotton (floss) as listed in the key – 1 skein of each colour and 2 skeins of 472 and 581

Stitch Count
128h x 152w

Design Size
20.3 x 24.2cm (8 x 9½in)

Stitches
Whole cross stitch, half cross stitch, backstitch

Stitch the Scene. . .
Prepare your fabric for work and mark the centre point (see page 98). Follow the chart on pages 34–35 and work over one block of Aida, using two strands of stranded cotton for full and half cross stitches. Work backstitches with one strand. When all stitching is complete, mount and frame your picture.

Up the Apple Tree

Picking fruit from the wild is a timeless pleasure, whether it's risking a tumble from a tree to snatch that biggest, juiciest apple or scratched hands and blue-stained fingers from blackberrying.

USE THE SCENE. . .

Any of the designs in this chapter would look very pretty stitched on to a tote bag – perfect for carrying picnic items for a lazy afternoon in the garden. Ready-to-stitch linen tote bags are available from DMC in different sizes.

UP THE APPLE TREE

Fabric
16-count ivory Aida (DMC DC88 712), 35.5 x 30.5cm (14 x 12in)

Threads
DMC stranded cotton (floss) as listed in the key – 1 skein of each colour and 2 skeins of 3348

Stitch Count
144h x 112w

Design Size
23 x 18cm (9 x 7in)

Stitches
Whole cross stitch, half cross stitch, backstitch

Stitch the Scene. . .
Prepare your fabric for work and mark the centre point (see page 98). Follow the chart on pages 36–37 and work over one block of Aida, using two strands of stranded cotton for full and half cross stitches. Work backstitches with one strand. When all stitching is complete, mount and frame your picture.

On the Rosebud Swing

The garden swing – who doesn't remember this timeless, innocent pleasure? This utterly charming design could be given more texture by working some of the cross stitches as French knots (see instructions and diagrams below). The design would also be perfect for a photo album to hold memories of milestone childhood occasions.

ON THE ROSEBUD SWING

Fabric
16-count ivory Aida (DMC DC88 712), 35.5 x 30.5cm (14 x 12in)

Threads
DMC stranded cotton (floss) as listed in the key – 1 skein of each colour and 3 skeins of 3348

Stitch Count
143h x 112w

Design Size
23 x 18cm (9 x 7in)

Stitches
Whole cross stitch, half cross stitch, backstitch, French knots (optional)

Stitch the Scene. . .
Prepare your fabric for work and mark the centre point (see page 98). Follow the chart on pages 38–39 and work over one block of Aida, using two strands of stranded cotton for full and half cross stitches. Work backstitches with one strand. To bring extra texture to the design, you could work the cross stitches in the grass (3348) and the cross stitches of the swing ropes (347, 760, 3328 and 3348) as massed French knots instead, using two strands of thread. When all stitching is complete, mount and frame your picture.

 Remember when. . .?

We didn't need computer games or big-screen TVs but just a sturdy tree and a thick rope to swing from. Even more fun could be had if the rope swing overhung a pond or river, for then we could plunge from the swing into the water for a cooling dip.

Working French Knots

French knots are small stitches that are used to add detail or texture to a design. For bigger knots, add more strands of thread to the needle.

Use two strands of thread and bring the needle through to the front of the fabric and wind the thread around the needle twice. Begin to 'post' the needle partly through to the back, one thread or part of a block away from the entry point. (This will stop the stitch being pulled to the wrong side.) Gently pull the thread you have wound so that it sits snugly at the point where the needle enters the fabric. Pull the needle through to the back and you should have a perfect knot in position.

Herding the Geese

This little one is hoping to earn some pocket money by looking after the geese. In times gone by geese were kept for their eggs and special-occasion meals such as Christmas, with their feathers used for pillows and cushions.

HERDING THE GEESE

Fabric
16-count ivory Aida (DMC DC88 712), 30.5 x 25.5cm (12 x 10in)

Threads
DMC stranded cotton (floss) as listed in the key – 1 skein of each colour

Stitch Count
112h x 80w

Design Size
18 x 12.7cm (7 x 5in)

Stitches
Whole cross stitch, half cross stitch, backstitch

Stitch the Scene. . .
Prepare your fabric for work and mark the centre point (see page 98). Follow the chart opposite and work over one block of Aida, using two strands of stranded cotton for full and half cross stitches. Work backstitches with one strand. When stitching is complete, mount and frame your picture.

 Remember when. . .?

The countryside of the past was a quiet place with no cars, no machinery and no encroaching industry. The land extended for countless acres, with fields ploughed by sturdy Percheron or Shire horses. One such horse might take a day to plough an acre with a single-furrow plough.

Herding the Geese

DMC stranded cotton

Full cross stitch (2 strands)

◤ 304	334	◣ 666	898	✕ 3325	3770
• 312	— 413	I 720	O 3041	＋ 3705	• blanc
◢ 318	414	840	I 3042	3740	

Half cross stitch (2 strands)

3041	3347
3325	3348

Backstitch (1 strand)

— 413

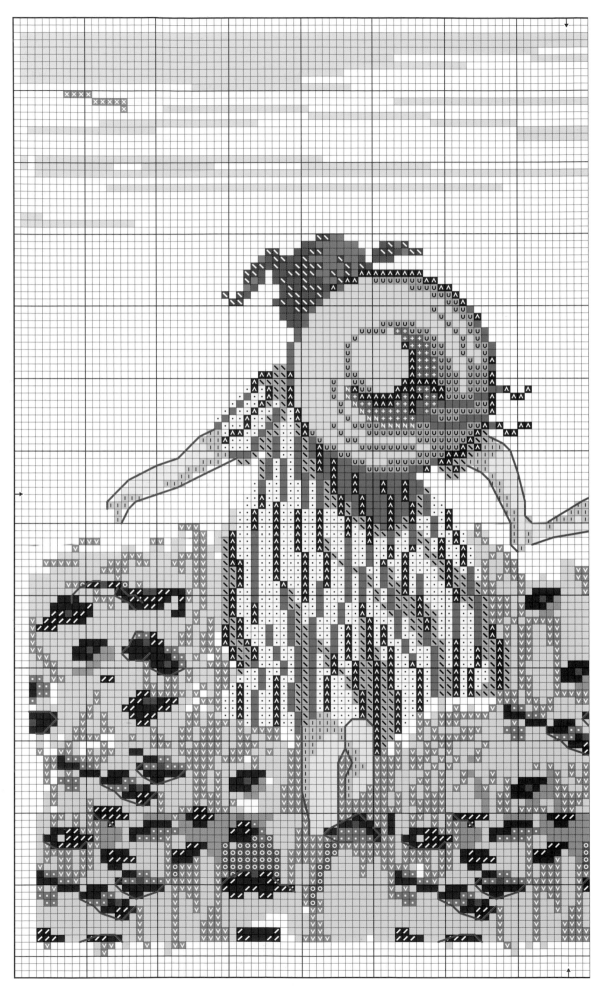

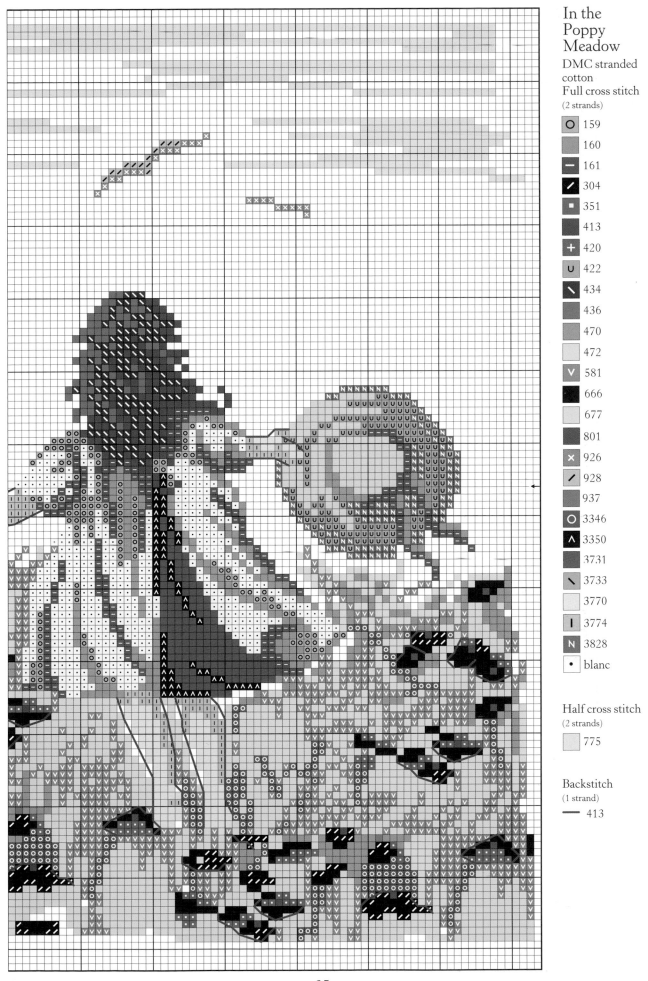

DMC stranded
cotton
Full cross stitch
(2 strands)

O	159
	160
−	161
/	304
▪	351
	413
+	420
U	422
╲	434
	436
	470
	472
V	581
	666
	677
	801
×	926
/	928
	937
O	3346
∧	3350
	3731
╲	3733
	3770
I	3774
N	3828
•	blanc

Half cross stitch
(2 strands)

	775

Backstitch
(1 strand)

−	413

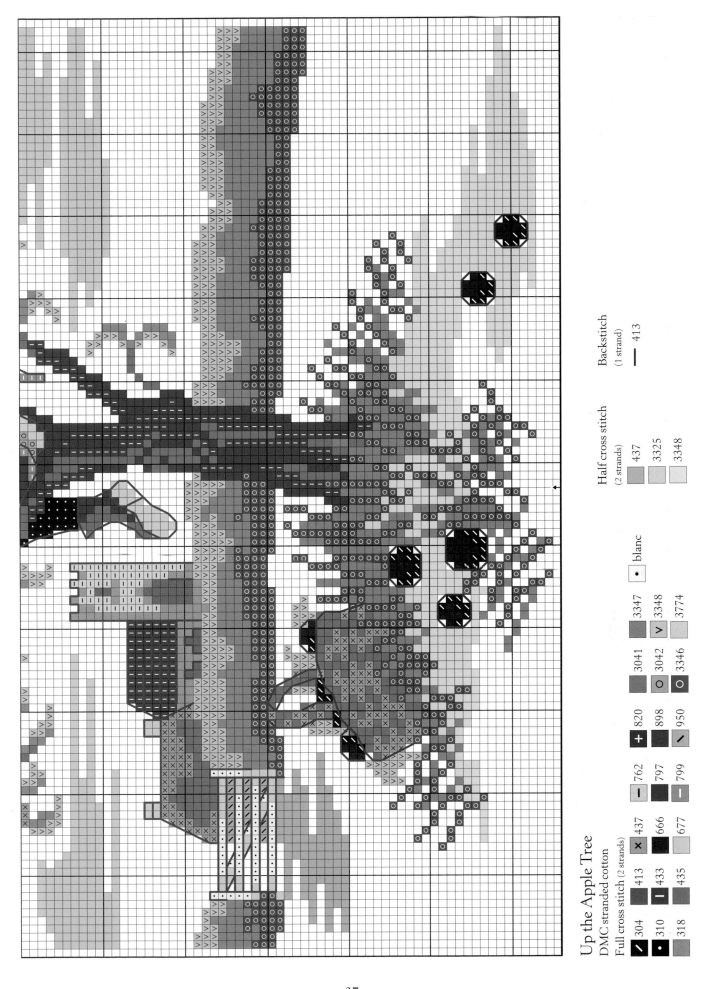

Up the Apple Tree
DMC stranded cotton
Full cross stitch (2 strands)

╱	304	✕	437
•	310	▬	666
▓	318	▪	433
		▒	435

▬	762	+	820
▬	797	▪	898
▬	799	╱	950

▒	3041	▪	3347
	3042	⊙	3348
⊙	3346		3774

•	blanc

Half cross stitch
(2 strands)

▒	437
▒	3325
▒	3348

Backstitch
(1 strand)

— 413

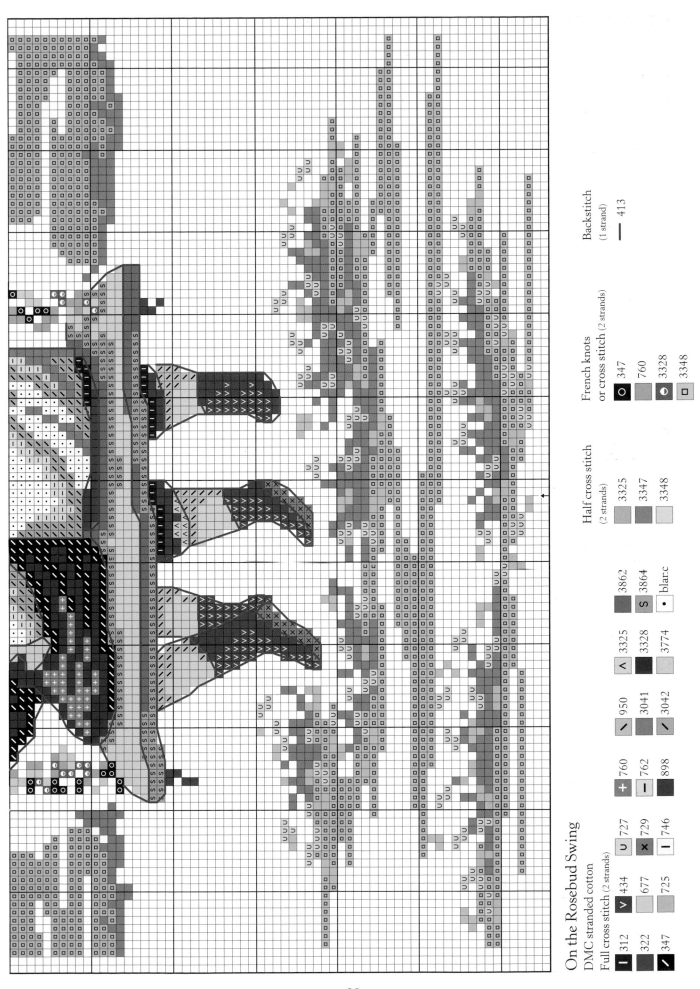

On the Rosebud Swing

DMC stranded cotton

Full cross stitch (2 strands)

▌	312	V	434	∪	727	
	322		677	×	729	
◿	347		725	I	746	

◿	950		3325		3862	
+	760	×	3328	S	3864
I	762	◿	3774	•	blarc
	898	◿	3041		
		◿	3042		

Half cross stitch
(2 strands)

	3325		3862
	3347		
	3348		

French knots
or cross stitch (2 strands)

●	347	◑	3328
	760	□	3348

Backstitch
(1 strand)

— 413

39

OUR BEST FRIEND

"How much is that doggie in the window?

The one with the waggley tail.

How much is that doggie in the window?

I do hope that doggie's for sale."

(Adapted from a Victorian music hall song)

Enlightened parents in the Victorian and Edwardian eras saw the value of having a dog in the family. Taking care of and playing with a dog, taught children to be kind and gentle to lesser creatures, to value the unconditional love a dog brings. The affectionate, fun-loving presence of this pet was in keeping with the Victorian attitude that childhood should preserve innocence and be spared the cares of the world.

No matter what the activity, a dog is guaranteed to join in. Children love to throw things; dogs love to retrieve – the perfect partnership. 'Go fetch!' might mean a stick or a stone or, better still, a ball – but perhaps not a balloon. A dog or puppy is a great companion for a walk in the countryside or a stroll along the beach, both places excellent for a good tug of war. Sometimes though these best of friends are tired from playing and need to sit on the warm sand together and just watch the boats sail by.

Go Fetch!

The simplest scene can tell a whole story. Dogs are loving companions and loyal friends but even the keenest pup would have difficulty retrieving a balloon!

Tug of War

These little girls are no match for their determined pet – tug of wars are his speciality!

GO FETCH! (PAGE 41)

GO FETCH! (PAGE 41)

Fabric
16-count ivory Aida (DMC DC88 712), 33 x 28cm (13 x 11in)

Threads
DMC stranded cotton (floss) as listed in the key –
1 skein of each colour

Stitch Count
123h x 93w

Design Size
19.5 x 14.8cm (7¾ x 5¾in)

Stitches
Whole cross stitch, half cross stitch, backstitch

Stitch the Scene. . .
Prepare your fabric for work and mark the centre point (see page 98). Follow the chart on page 44 and work over one block of Aida, using two strands of stranded cotton for full and half cross stitches. Work backstitches with one strand. When all stitching is complete, mount and frame your picture.

TUG OF WAR

Fabric
16-count ivory Aida (DMC DC88 712), 25.5 x 33cm (10 x 13in)

Threads
DMC stranded cotton (floss) as listed in the key –
1 skein of each colour

Stitch Count
84h x 120w

Design Size
13.4 x 19cm (5¼ x 7½in)

Stitches
Whole cross stitch, half cross stitch, backstitch

Stitch the Scene. . .
Prepare your fabric for work and mark the centre point (see page 98). Follow the chart on pages 46–47 and work over one block of Aida, using two strands of stranded cotton for full and half cross stitches. Work backstitches with one strand. When all stitching is complete, mount and frame your picture.

Me and My Dog

This utterly charming little scene could be stitched as a birthday card, perhaps omitting the sea and boats background and using one of the alphabets on page 97 to stitch the child's name and age. To make the design smaller, work it on 18-count Aida.

ME AND MY DOG

Fabric
16-count ivory Aida (DMC DC88 712), 30.5 x 28cm (12 x 11in)

Threads
DMC stranded cotton (floss) as listed in the key – 1 skein of each colour

Stitch Count
113h x 88w

Design Size
18 x 14cm (7 x 5½in)

Stitches
Whole cross stitch, half cross stitch, backstitch

Stitch the Scene. . .
Prepare your fabric for work and mark the centre point (see page 98). Follow the chart on page 45 and work over one block of Aida, using two strands of stranded cotton for full and half cross stitches. Work backstitches with one strand. When all stitching is complete, mount and frame your picture.

USE THE SCENE. . .

This sweet design would make an attractive bedroom door sign for a little boy, perhaps with the child's name stitched below the design using one of the alphabets on page 97. You could stitch the whole design or just the boy and his dog.

Go Fetch!

DMC stranded cotton

Full cross stitch (2 strands)

— 304	∧ 334	■ 666	v 950	+ 3325	☐ 3774		◆ 322	☐ 3042
╱ 312	■ 413	☐ 677	O 3743	• blanc			I 677	☐ 3325
■ 322	■ 435	— 729	╲ 3042					

Half cross stitch (2 strands)

Backstitch (1 strand) — 413

Me and My Dog
DMC stranded cotton

Full cross stitch (2 strands)				Half cross stitch (2 strands)		Backstitch (1 strand)
▬ 304	677	✕ 840	⊙ 3743	312	3042	— 413
✓ 312	— 729	❘ 3041	3770	❘ 677	3325	
322	780	❙ 3042	∨ 3774	729	╱ 3770	
666	839	✚ 3325	• blanc	3041		

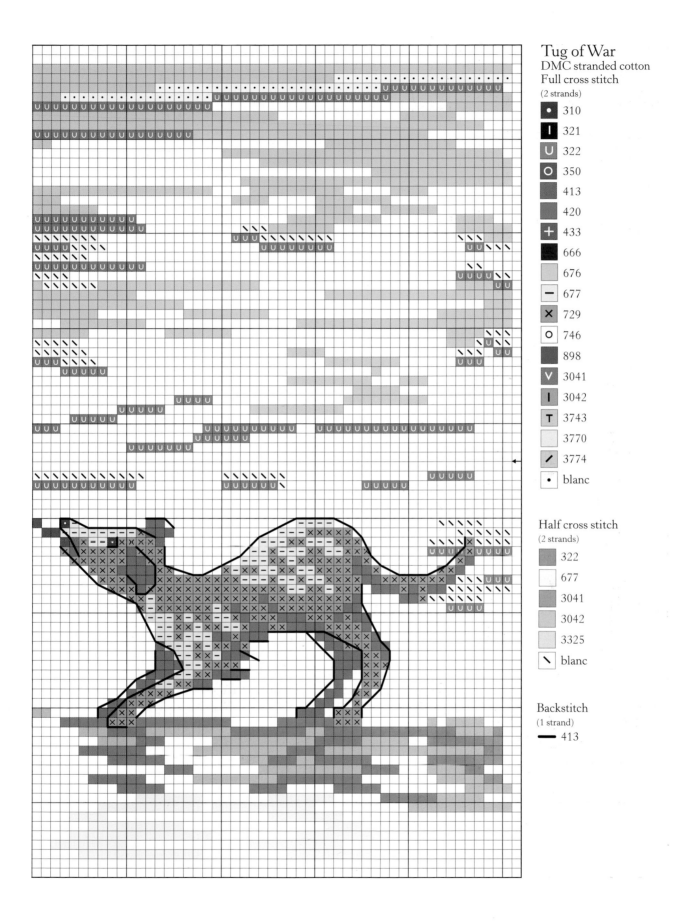

Tug of War

DMC stranded cotton

Full cross stitch
(2 strands)

•	310
I	321
U	322
O	350
	413
	420
+	433
	666
	676
–	677
X	729
O	746
	898
V	3041
I	3042
T	3743
	3770
/	3774
•	blanc

Half cross stitch
(2 strands)

	322
	677
	3041
	3042
	3325
\	blanc

Backstitch
(1 strand)

—	413

SCHOOLYARD GAMES

❝Oranges and lemons,
Say the bells of St Clement's.
You owe me five farthings,
Say the bells of St Martin's.❞

(Traditional nursery rhyme)

How many of us remember playing Oranges and Lemons at school, running through an arch created by two children and hoping we wouldn't be caught when the arch fell at the end of the song? Most of us have strong memories of our school days and in particular the games we played with our friends at break times. There was much enjoyment to be had from street games, such as leap frog, conkers, jacks and hoops. Skipping games were great fun, especially those with a song, such as 'salt, mustard, vinegar, pepper'. Hopscotch has long been a very popular game, testing hopping and jumping skills in a numbered grid chalked on the playground.

Traditional games involving large groups of children were an exciting part of schoolyard activities, and hide and seek, follow the leader, tag and statues were played regularly, and were often more fun if the teacher joined in, especially if you could persuade her to be 'seeker' each time.

Play Time with Teacher

Yesterday's games only needed a few friends and some space to run around in. Playing with teacher was fun, especially Ring-a-Ring of Roses or Please Mr Crocodile.

Follow the Leader

Are these little ones about to play a traditional game of Follow the Leader or are the girls planning some mischief? The design would also make an adorable greetings card.

PLAY TIME WITH TEACHER (PAGE 49)

Fabric
16-count ivory Aida (DMC DC88 712), 35.5 × 40.5cm (14 × 16in)

Threads
DMC stranded cotton (floss) as listed in the key – 1 skein of each colour and 2 skeins each of 3035, 3042 and blanc

Stitch Count
140h × 170w

Design Size
22.2 × 27cm (8¾ × 10¾in)

Stitches
Whole cross stitch, half cross stitch, backstitch

Stitch the Scene. . .
Prepare your fabric for work and mark the centre point (see page 98). Follow the chart on pages 54–55 and work over one block of Aida, using two strands of stranded cotton for full and half cross stitches. Work backstitches with one strand. When all stitching is complete, mount and frame your picture.

FOLLOW THE LEADER

Fabric
16-count ivory Aida (DMC DC88 712), 23 × 28cm (9 × 11in)

Threads
DMC stranded cotton (floss) as listed in the key – 1 skein of each colour

Stitch Count
56h × 95w

Design Size
9 × 15cm (3½ × 6in)

Stitches
Whole cross stitch, half cross stitch, backstitch

Stitch the Scene. . .
Prepare your fabric for work and mark the centre point (see page 98). Follow the chart on page 52 and work over one block of Aida, using two strands of stranded cotton for full and half cross stitches. Work backstitches with one strand. When all stitching is complete, mount and frame your picture.

Come Skip with Me

Nothing epitomizes the joy of childhood quite like skipping games and they have been a traditional element of schoolyard games for centuries. Skip with your best friend or with a whole group – either way is fun.

COME SKIP WITH ME

Fabric
16-count ivory Aida (DMC DC88 712), 30.5 x 25.5cm (12 x 10in)

Threads
DMC stranded cotton (floss) as listed in the key – 1 skein of each colour

Stitch Count
112h x 80w

Design Size
18 x 12.7cm (7 x 5in)

Stitches
Whole cross stitch, half cross stitch, backstitch

Stitch the Scene. . .
Prepare your fabric for work and mark the centre point (see page 98). Follow the chart on page 53 and work over one block of Aida, using two strands of stranded cotton for full and half cross stitches. Work backstitches with one strand. When all stitching is complete, mount and frame your picture.

 Remember when. . .?

You had to line up in the playground and be absolutely silent before being allowed to go into class – and how the chatter died away much more quickly on a cold, wet day.

Follow the Leader

DMC stranded cotton

Full cross stitch (2 strands)

■ 304	□ 677	▨ 841	▨ 3042
▨ 310	▨ 680	▨ 898	▨ 3705
▨ 413	○ 746	I 950	▨ 3774
╱ 666	L 840	▨ 3041	• blanc

Half cross stitch (2 strands)

— 677

╲ 3042

Backstitch (1 strand)

— 413

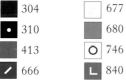 **Remember when. . .?**

School desks were all made of wood (much ink-stained, chipped and carved with names), each with an inkwell set into the wooden frame and a lift-up, hinged lid you had to be careful not to bang shut during lesson time.

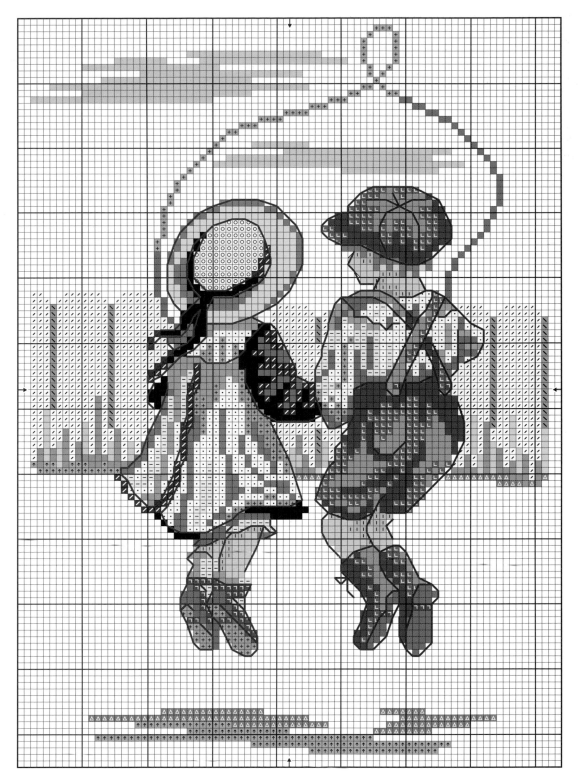

Come Skip with Me
DMC stranded cotton

Full cross stitch (2 strands)

+ 318	680	I 950
321	O 746	3041
⌐ 413	− 762	3042
414	L 840	3705
╱ 666	841	3774
677	898	• blanc

Half cross stitch (2 strands)

╲ 841	3347
△ 3041	3348
↑ 3042	╱ blanc
3325	

Backstitch (1 strand)

— 413

Play Time with Teacher
DMC stranded cotton
Full cross stitch (2 strands)

●	310	Y	746
V	312	∧	869
╱	321	I	898
	322	╲	930
	336	╲	931
⌐	351	↑	932
+	413		950
▲	420	▫	3041
	422	⌐	3042
⋋	433	╱	3325
○	435	V	3348
▫	498	I	3743
	666	L	3750
–	676		3770
	677	╲	3774
■	680	•	blanc
✕	729		

Half cross stitch (2 strands)

	317		898
	415		3041
	434		3042
○	435		3325
	436		3348
	762	⊙	blanc

Backstitch (1 strand)
— 413
— 632

55

FUN AT THE BEACH

Who doesn't recall the childhood delights of the seaside, when all you needed was a bucket, a spade and a mile of sand. The lure of the seaside has long been an enduring one but it wasn't always so; not until the mid 19th century did the health spas gradually become holiday places for people to escape to.

For adults, modesty and decorum could not be left behind in the towns though. Seaside fashions were slightly more relaxed but bathing machines were still being used during the early Edwardian period. Bathers had to be suitably, voluminously attired – no single-minded quest for the perfect tan in those days. Gradually though mixed bathing became more acceptable and bathing machines disappeared, many replaced by the colourful huts that still adorn many beaches.

For children, the magnet was the sea. At the water's edge they passed hours in absorbing pastimes – shrimping, collecting shells and pebbles and building sandcastles. For the more adventurous there were donkey rides along the beach, wading in rock pools to discover all manner of fascinating creatures or racing among the dunes to catch enough breeze to fly a kite.

Fun in the Sand

Yesterday's children had no need for noisy amusement arcades or powered water sports – just a bucket and spade was enough for hours of fun.

Fun in the Sand

No trip to the beach was complete without a sturdy bucket and spade – the only tools needed for hours of simple fun in the golden sand. This design would look great stitched on to a beach bag.

FUN IN THE SAND (PAGE 57)

Fabric
16-count ivory Aida (DMC DC88 712), 30.5 x 25.5cm (12 x 10in)

Threads
DMC stranded cotton (floss) as listed in the key – 1 skein of each colour

Stitch Count
112h x 80w

Design Size
18 x 12.7cm (7 x 5in)

Stitches
Whole cross stitch, half cross stitch, backstitch

Stitch the Scene. . .
Prepare your fabric for work and mark the centre point (see page 98). Follow the chart on page 62 and work over one block of Aida, using two strands of stranded cotton for full and half cross stitches. Work backstitches with one strand. When all stitching is complete, mount and frame your picture.

Fun at the Rock Pool

If a bucket and spade were essential, a net came in handy too, to capture and study strange creatures from warm rock pools.

FUN AT THE ROCK POOL

Fabric
16-count ivory Aida (DMC DC88 712), 18 x 15.3cm (7 x 6in)

Threads
DMC stranded cotton (floss) as listed in the key – 1 skein of each colour

Stitch Count
60h x 47w

Design Size
9.5 x 7.6cm (3¾ x 3in)

Stitches
Whole cross stitch, half cross stitch, backstitch

Stitch the Scene. . .
Prepare your fabric for work and mark the centre point (see page 98). Follow the chart on page 64 and work over one block of Aida, using two strands of stranded cotton for full and half cross stitches. Work backstitches with one strand. When all stitching is complete, mount into a double-fold card – see page 101 for instructions.

Flying Our Kites

Even on the hottest of days there was usually some off-shore breeze to stir a kite into action, and if not it was still fun racing along the sand with friends. You could stitch just one of these exuberant boys for a birthday card.

FLYING OUR KITES

Fabric
16-count ivory Aida (DMC DC88 712)
28 × 33cm (11 × 13in)

Threads
DMC stranded cotton (floss) as listed in the key – 1 skein of each colour

Stitch Count
85h × 118w

Design Size
13.5 × 18.5cm (5½ × 7½in)

Stitches
Whole cross stitch, half cross stitch, backstitch

Stitch the Scene. . .
Prepare your fabric for work and mark the centre point (see page 98). Follow the chart on page 63 and work over one block of Aida, using two strands of stranded cotton for full and half cross stitches. Work backstitches with one strand. When all stitching is complete, mount and frame your picture.

Fun in the Water

That first dash from the hot sand into the cool water, hat flying, petticoats awry, was the best fun! Instead of making up as a card, frame the design as a little picture.

FUN IN THE WATER

Fabric
16-count ivory Aida (DMC DC88 712)
18 × 15.3cm (7 × 6in)

Threads
DMC stranded cotton (floss) as listed in the key – 1 skein of each colour

Stitch Count
53h × 46w

Design Size
8.5 × 7.2cm (3½ × 2¾in)

Stitches
Whole cross stitch, half cross stitch, backstitch

Stitch the Scene. . .
Prepare your fabric for work and mark the centre point (see page 98). Follow the chart on page 64 and work over one block of Aida, using two strands of stranded cotton for full and half cross stitches. Work backstitches with one strand. When all stitching is complete, mount on the front of a single-fold card – see page 100.

SPLASHING FUN

Fabric
16-count ivory Aida (DMC DC88 712), 12.7 × 25.5cm (5 × 10in)

Threads
DMC stranded cotton (floss) as listed in the key – 1 skein of each colour. 1 skein of perlé cotton No. 5 (colour code 666) for a tassel

Stitch Count
32h × 112

Design Size
5 × 18cm (2 × 7in)

Stitches
Whole cross stitch, half cross stitch, backstitch

Stitch the Scene. . .
Prepare your fabric for work and mark the centre point (see page 98). Follow the chart on page 65 and work over one block of Aida, using two strands of stranded cotton for full and half cross stitches. Work backstitches with one strand. When all stitching is complete, make up as a bookmark (see page 101) and add a tassel (page 102).

Splashing Fun

The water's edge was a magnet, whether you were tiptoeing into the water to collect shrimps in a bucket or simply jumping over waves. Why not make this bookmark for your holiday reading?

Making Sandcastles

Bucket + spade + sand = sandcastles: there is no simpler equation. For boys, an impressive fort could be created; for girls, the castle of a fairy princess.

Instead of using this simple little design on an album cover, it could be used as a patch to adorn many ready-made items, such as a sun hat.

MAKING SANDCASTLES

Fabric
16-count ivory Aida (DMC DC88 712)
7.6 × 7.6cm (3 × 3in)

Threads
DMC stranded cotton (floss) as listed in the key – 1 skein of each colour

Stitch Count
21h × 21w

Design Size
3.3 × 3.3cm (1½ × 1½in)

Stitches
Whole cross stitch, half cross stitch, backstitch

Stitch the Scene. . .
Prepare your fabric for work and mark the centre point (see page 98). Follow the chart on page 65 and work over one block of Aida, using two strands of stranded cotton for full and half cross stitches. Work backstitches with one strand. When all stitching is complete, prepare your embroidery as a patch and attach to your photo album (see page 100).

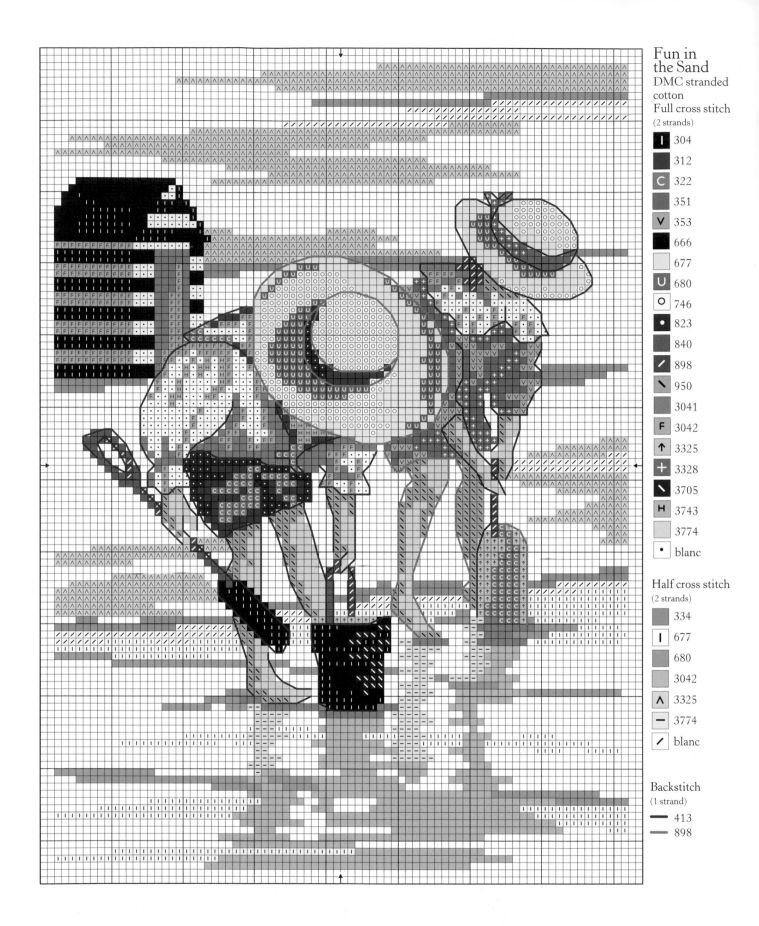

Fun in
the Sand
DMC stranded
cotton
Full cross stitch
(2 strands)

I	304
	312
C	322
	351
V	353
	666
	677
U	680
O	746
•	823
	840
/	898
\	950
	3041
F	3042
↑	3325
+	3328
\	3705
H	3743
	3774
•	blanc

Half cross stitch
(2 strands)

	334
I	677
	680
	3042
∧	3325
−	3774
/	blanc

Backstitch
(1 strand)

| — | 413 |
| — | 898 |

Flying Our Kites

DMC stranded cotton

Full cross stitch (2 strands)

⊃	950			⊐	3041
⊢	3042			✕	3325
	3345			▌	3347
	3348				3774
O	3801			•	blanc

▬	304			•	310
╱	311			✛	322
	415				433
■	666			▎	677
╎	729			O	746
╲	898				

Half cross stitch (2 strands)

	322			←	677
	729				3042
	3325			╲	blanc

Backstitch (1 strand)

—	413

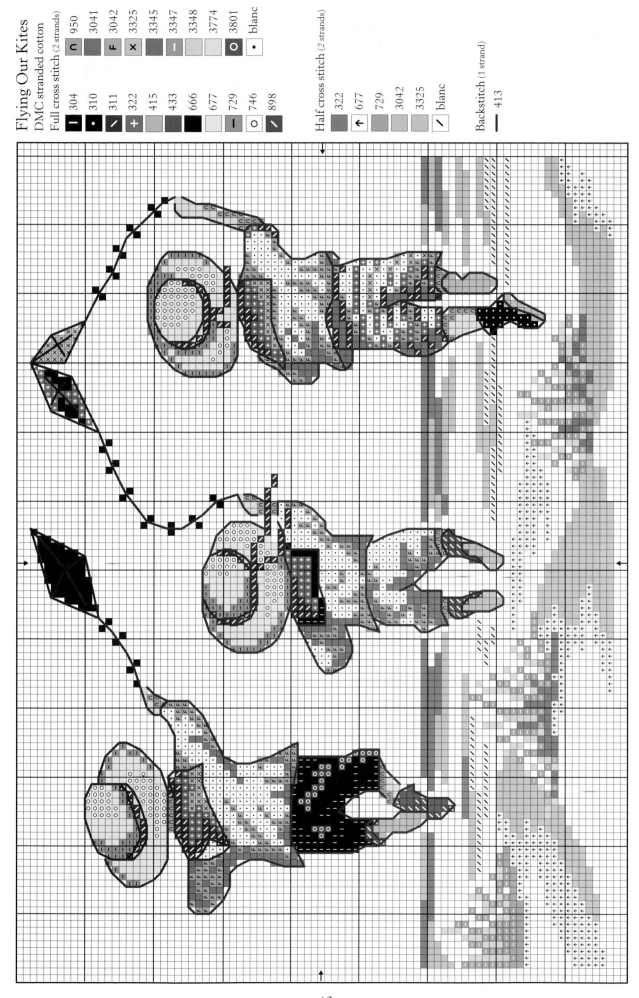

63

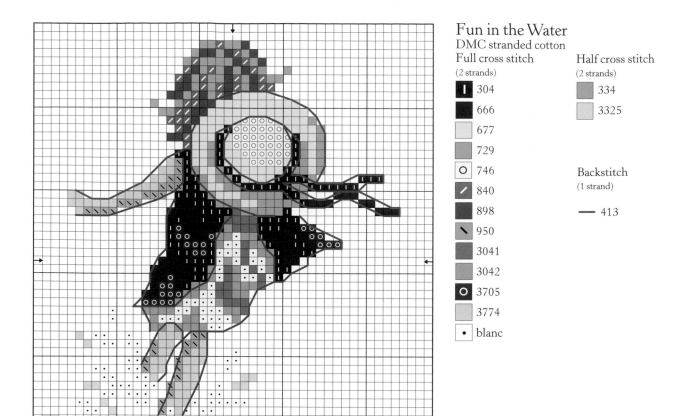

Fun in the Water

DMC stranded cotton

Full cross stitch
(2 strands)

I	304
	666
	677
	729
O	746
/	840
	898
\	950
	3041
	3042
O	3705
	3774
•	blanc

Half cross stitch
(2 strands)

	334
	3325

Backstitch
(1 strand)

— 413

Fun at the Rock Pool

DMC stranded cotton

Full cross stitch
(2 strands)

I	304
	312
	318
+	334
	666
×	720
	729
/	840
	898
\	950
	3041
	3042
I	3325
	3774
•	blanc

Half cross stitch
(2 strands)

	334
O	746
	3325

Backstitch
(1 strand)

— 413

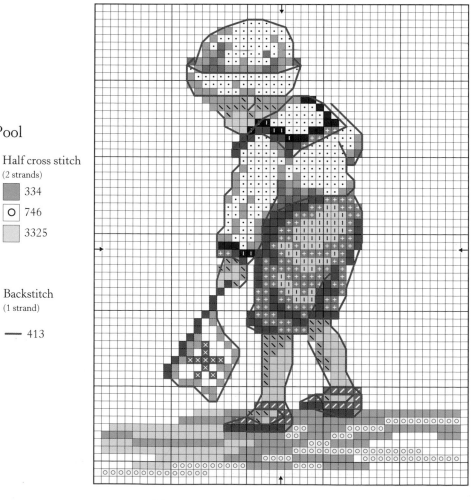

Splashing Fun
DMC stranded cotton

Full cross stitch
(2 strands)

I	304
■	312
+	334
×	435
■	666
□	677
■	729
O	746
■	839
****	950
■	3041
■	3042
I	3325
O	3705
■	3774
·	blanc

Half cross stitch
(2 strands)

■	334
∕	677
U	950

Backstitch
(1 strand)

—	413

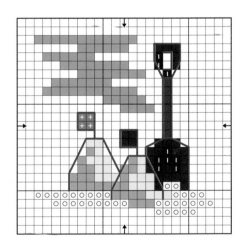

Making Sandcastles
DMC stranded cotton

Full cross stitch
(2 strands)

I	304
+	334
■	434
■	666
□	677
■	729

Half cross stitch
(2 strands)

■	334
O	677

Backstitch
(1 strand)

—	413

AND SO TO BED

" *Twinkle, twinkle little star,*
How I wonder what you are.
Up above the world so high,
Like a diamond in the sky. "

(Song lyrics by Jane Taylor, 1806)

*I*t is night and the house is cosy and quiet but with dark pools devoid of lamplight. The favourite toy is already clutched in small arms and that circle of light around the bed is inviting. Soon mummy or daddy will open the pages of a book and their voice will bring a favourite story to life. You will have them all to yourself as they create a world for you – be the conspirator during the funny bits and the guardian during the scary bits. And soon the magical world of the story will blur as eyelids drop and breathing steadies.

The bedtime story is timeless. It might be Harry Potter, Willie Wonka or the BFG today but traditional favourites still endure.

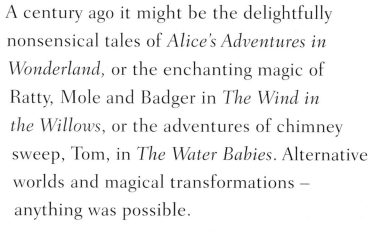

A century ago it might be the delightfully nonsensical tales of *Alice's Adventures in Wonderland,* or the enchanting magic of Ratty, Mole and Badger in *The Wind in the Willows,* or the adventures of chimney sweep, Tom, in *The Water Babies*. Alternative worlds and magical transformations – anything was possible.

Ready For Story Time

The bed is warm, the sheets and drapes smell sweet, it has been an exciting day and story time is coming: bedtime isn't so bad after all.

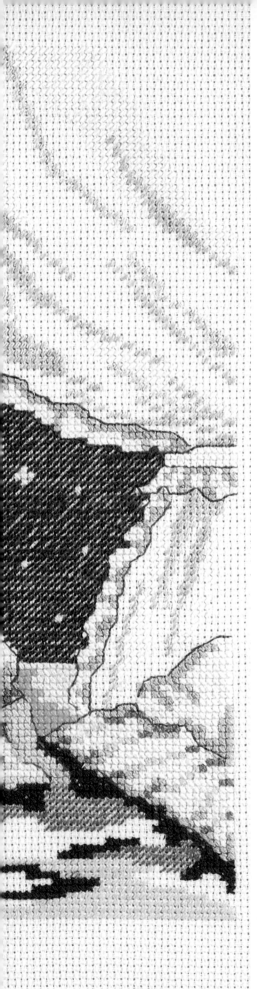

Ready for Story Time

Story time is the moment that makes bedtime bearable. Ready for bed in their nightgowns and caps, these little ones wonder what magical world they will visit tonight.

USE THE SCENE. . .

This bedtime scene would look lovely made up into a nightdress case. After the embroidery is complete, hem the edges of the Aida and sew it on to a simple case and then edge it with a decorative trim.

READY FOR STORY TIME

Fabric
16-count ivory Aida (DMC DC88 712), 33 × 38cm (13 × 15in)

Threads
DMC stranded cotton (floss) as listed in the key – 1 skein of each colour and 2 skeins of 3042 and 3325 and 3 skeins of 312 and blanc

Stitch Count
128h × 160w

Design Size
20.3 × 25.5cm (8 × 10in)

Stitches
Whole cross stitch, half cross stitch, backstitch

Stitch the Scene. . .
Prepare your fabric for work and mark the centre point (see page 98). Follow the chart overleaf and work over one block of Aida, using two strands of stranded cotton for full and half cross stitches. Work backstitches with one strand. When all stitching is complete, mount and frame your picture.

I LOVE MY TEDDY BEAR

Fabric
Teddy with bib (DMC code GN001L)

Threads
DMC stranded cotton (floss) as listed in the key – scraps of each

Stitch Count
15h × 19w

Design Size
2.5 × 3cm (1 × 1⅛in)

Stitches
Whole cross stitch, backstitch

Stitch the Scene. . .
Find the centre point on the bib and follow the chart overleaf, working over one block of Aida, using two strands of stranded cotton for full cross stitches and one strand for backstitches.

I Love My Teddy Bear

The teddy bear is now over a century old and still a much-loved toy. This motif has been worked on teddy's bib but you could stitch it as a card.

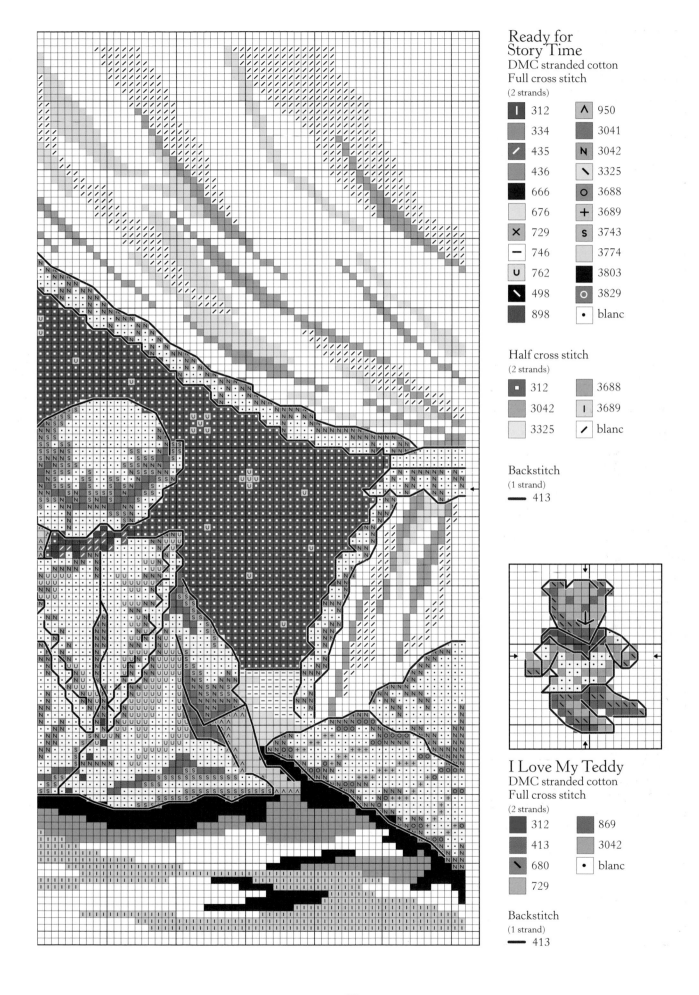

Ready for Story Time
DMC stranded cotton
Full cross stitch
(2 strands)

I	312	∧	950
	334		3041
∕	435	N	3042
	436	＼	3325
	666	O	3688
	676	+	3689
×	729	S	3743
−	746		3774
U	762		3803
＼	498	O	3829
	898	·	blanc

Half cross stitch
(2 strands)

▪	312		3688
	3042	I	3689
	3325	∕	blanc

Backstitch
(1 strand)
— 413

I Love My Teddy
DMC stranded cotton
Full cross stitch
(2 strands)

	312		869
	413		3042
＼	680	·	blanc
	729		

Backstitch
(1 strand)
— 413

Messing About in Boats

Bobbing about in a boat with friends for a spot of fishing or swimming must be one of the most perfect ways to spend an afternoon.

MESSING ABOUT IN BOATS (PAGE 73)

Fabric
16-count ivory Aida (DMC DC88 712), 30.5 × 35.5cm (12 × 14in)

Threads
DMC stranded cotton (floss) as listed in the key – 1 skein of each colour and 2 skeins of 3325

Stitch Count
101h × 146w

Design Size
16 × 23cm (6½ × 9in)

Stitches
Whole cross stitch, half cross stitch, backstitch

Stitch the Scene. . .
Prepare your fabric for work and mark the centre point (see page 98). Follow the chart overleaf and work over one block of Aida, using two strands of stranded cotton for full and half cross stitches. Work backstitches with one strand. When all stitching is complete, mount and frame your picture.

Me and My Boat

The little boy in this charming little design looks unsure as to whether he should his risk his beloved toy boat in the rough sea after all. If stitched on Aida band, the design could also be used to decorate an album or journal.

ME AND MY BOAT

Fabric
16-count ivory Aida (DMC DC88 712), 25.5 × 12.7cm (10 × 5in)

Threads
DMC stranded cotton (floss) as listed in the key – 1 skein of each colour; 1 skein of perlé cotton No.5 (colour code 666) for a tassel

Stitch Count
112h × 32w

Design Size
18 × 5cm (7 × 2in)

Stitches
Whole cross stitch, half cross stitch, backstitch

Stitch the Scene. . .
Prepare your fabric for work and mark the centre point (see page 98). Follow the chart on page 79 and work over one block of Aida, using two strands of stranded cotton for full and half cross stitches. Work backstitches with one strand. When all stitching is complete, make up as a bookmark (see page 101) and add a tassel (page 102).

Gone Fishing

This sweet little boy waiting patiently for a fish to take his bait makes a lovely greetings card. The motif could also be used to adorn a bag for swimwear, perhaps adding a child's name using one of the alphabets on page 97.

GONE FISHING

Fabric
16-count ivory Aida (DMC DC88 712), 15 x 15cm (6 x 6in)

Threads
DMC stranded cotton (floss) as listed in the key –
1 skein of each colour

Stitch Count
48h x 45w

Design Size
7.6 x 7.3cm (3 x 2¾in)

Stitches
Whole cross stitch, half cross stitch, backstitch

Stitch the Scene. . .
Prepare your fabric for work and mark the centre point (see page 98). Follow the chart on page 78 and work over one block of Aida, using two strands of stranded cotton for full and half cross stitches. Work backstitches with one strand. When all stitching is complete, mount into a double-fold card – see page 101 for instructions.

Maiden Voyage

A splendid wooden sailing boat complete with linen sails could provide hours of fun at the seaside or even on the ornamental pond in the garden.

MAIDEN VOYAGE

Fabric
16-count ivory Aida (DMC DC88 712), 18 x 15cm (7 x 6in)

Threads
DMC stranded cotton (floss) as listed in the key – 1 skein of each colour

Stitch Count
61h x 46w

Design Size
9.7 x 7.3cm (3¾ x 2¾in)

Stitches
Whole cross stitch, half cross stitch, backstitch

Stitch the Scene. . .
Prepare your fabric for work and mark the centre point (see page 98). Follow the chart on page 78 and work over one block of Aida, using two strands of stranded cotton for full and half cross stitches. Work backstitches with one strand. When all stitching is complete, mount into a double-fold card – see page 101 for instructions.

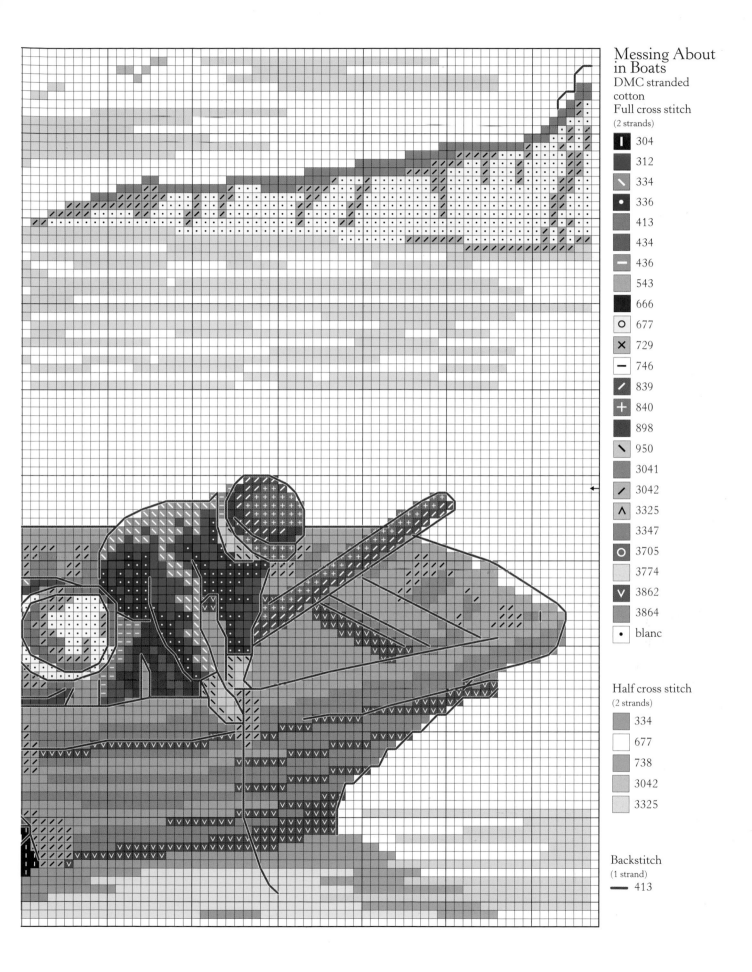

Messing About
in Boats

DMC stranded
cotton

Full cross stitch
(2 strands)

Symbol	Colour
I	304
	312
\	334
•	336
	413
	434
−	436
	543
	666
O	677
X	729
−	746
/	839
+	840
	898
\	950
	3041
/	3042
∧	3325
	3347
O	3705
	3774
V	3862
	3864
•	blanc

Half cross stitch
(2 strands)

Symbol	Colour
	334
	677
	738
	3042
	3325

Backstitch
(1 strand)

Symbol	Colour
—	413

Maiden Voyage
DMC stranded cotton

Full cross stitch (2 strands)		Half cross stitch (2 strands)	
■	304	▨	800
I	349	▨	3325
▨	351		
▨	676		
O	677	**Backstitch** (1 strand)	
×	729	—	413
▨	840		
—	841		
▨	3041		
\	3042		
▨	3743		
▨	3770		
/	3774		
•	blanc		

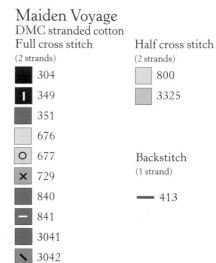

Gone Fishing
DMC stranded cotton

Full cross stitch (2 strands)		Half cross stitch (2 strands)	
▨	312	/	677
\	334	▨	3042
▨	407		
▨	677		
O	729	**Backstitch** (1 strand)	
▨	869	—	413
V	3041		
▨	3042		
▨	3325		
—	3743		
▨	3774		
•	blanc		

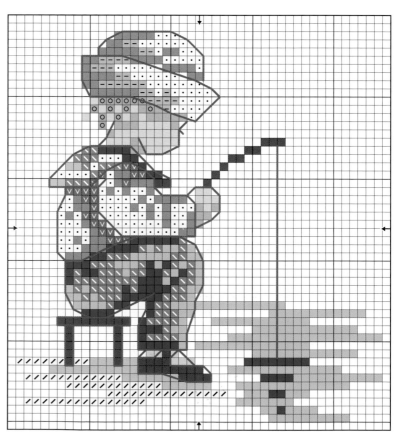

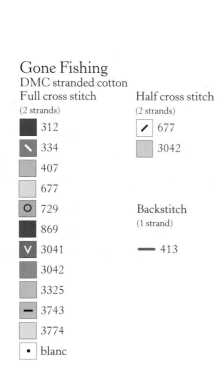

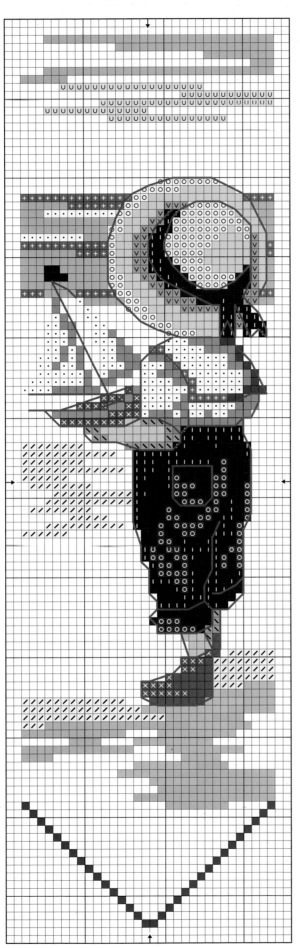

Me and My Boat

DMC stranded cotton

Full cross stitch (2 strands)		Half cross stitch (2 strands)	
I	304	╱	677
	312		729
+	334		3042
×	435		3325
	437	U	3774
	666		
	677		
V	729		**Backstitch** (1 strand)
O	746		
	801	──	413
╲	950		
	3042		
O	3705		
	3774		
•	blanc		

Remember when. . .?

No proper lady or gentleman was seen hatless during the 19th and 20th centuries. Even when relaxing at the weekends or while on holiday, hats would still be worn, though were slightly less formal. The straw boater, often called a skimmer, was a favourite with men, woman and children alike.

CHRISTMAS WONDERS

" Christmas is coming, the goose is getting fat.

Please put a penny in the old man's hat.

If you haven't got a penny, a ha'penny will do.

If you haven't got a ha'penny, a farthing will do.

If you haven't got a farthing, then God bless you. "

(Traditional song)

Before the Victorian re-invention of Christmas there were no Christmas trees, no crackers, no card giving, no Christmas cake and few presents. The Victorians transformed the hotchpotch that was Christmas into a wonderful, fun-filled occasion that celebrated family, friends and goodwill to those less fortunate.

Christmas became a time for children, and by the Edwardian period they looked forward to a visit from Father Christmas or Santa Claus, entering his magical world of reindeers and sleigh by sending letters asking for their heart's desire and hoping for lots of presents around the tree on Christmas morning.

In northern climates, another of the pleasures of Yuletide is the possibility of ice and snow, with all the fun to be had from a white winter wonderland – snowball fights, building snowmen, tobogganing and ice skating.

Letters to Santa

Yesterday's Christmas was filled with nostalgic romance – a promise of sweet treats, family pleasures and fun in the snow, and of course a visit from Santa in answer to your letter.

With Love at Christmas

Since Victorian times the giving and receiving of presents has become an increasingly important part of Christmas – but sometimes the simplest of gifts given with love are more than enough.

WITH LOVE AT CHRISTMAS

Fabric
16-count ivory Aida (DMC DC88 712), 25.5 × 30.5cm (10 × 12in)

Threads
DMC stranded cotton (floss) and Light Effects as listed in the key – 1 skein of each colour

Stitch Count
112h × 80w

Design Size
12.7 × 18cm (5 × 7in)

Stitches
Whole cross stitch, half cross stitch, backstitch

Stitch the Scene. . .
Prepare your fabric for work and mark the centre point (see page 98). Follow the chart on page 86 and work over one block of Aida, using two strands of stranded cotton for full and half cross stitches. Work backstitches with one strand. When stitching is complete, mount and frame your picture.

Letters to Santa

This charming snowy scene, with the old-fashioned post box, shows two children eager to send their letters to Father Christmas. You could also stitch this scene to decorate a box containing a stock of Christmas cards.

LETTERS TO SANTA (PAGE 81)

Fabric
16-count ivory Aida (DMC DC88 712), 38 × 33cm (15 × 13in)

Threads
DMC stranded cotton (floss) as listed in the key – 1 skein of each colour and 2 skeins of 677 and 762

Stitch Count
159h × 127w

Design Size
25.5 × 20cm (10 × 8in)

Stitche
Whole cross stitch, three-quarter cross stitch, half cross stitch, backstitch

Stitch the Scene. . .
Prepare fabric for work and mark the centre (see page 98). Follow the chart on pages 88–89 and work over one block of Aida, using two strands of stranded cotton for full and half cross stitches. Work backstitches with one strand. When stitching is complete, mount and frame.

Ice Skating Friends

Let it snow, let it snow, let it snow! If you live in chillier climes, the icing on
the cake at Christmas time has to be snow. This scene would make a charming
Christmas card, especially if worked on a sparkly DMC Golden Aida.

ICE SKATING FRIENDS

Fabric
16-count ivory Aida (DMC DC88 712), 25.5 x 30.5cm (10 x 12in)

Threads
DMC stranded cotton (floss) as listed in the key – 1 skein of each colour

Stitch Count
77h x 112w

Design Size
12.3 x 18cm (4¾ x 7in)

Stitches
Whole cross stitch, half cross stitch, backstitch

Stitch the Scene. . .
Prepare your fabric for work and mark the centre point (see page 98). Follow the chart on
page 87 and work over one block of Aida, using two strands of stranded cotton for full and half
cross stitches. Work backstitches with one strand. When stitching is complete, mount and frame.

Oh, Christmas Tree

Since Victorian times, decorating the tree at Christmas time has become a favourite tradition in many families. This nostalgic design uses Light Effects threads to bring extra sparkle to the tree. Why not stitch just the children and the tree on 18-count Aida for a Christmas card?

OH, CHRISTMAS TREE

Fabric
16-count ivory Aida (DMC DC88 712), 25.5 x 30.5cm (10 x 12in)

Threads
DMC stranded cotton (floss) as listed in the key – 1 skein of each colour and 2 skeins of blanc; DMC Light Effects as listed in the key

Stitch Count
112h x 80w

Design Size
12.7 x 18cm (5 x 7in)

Stitches
Whole cross stitch, half cross stitch, backstitch

Stitch the Scene. . .
Prepare fabric for work and mark the centre (see page 98). Follow the chart opposite and work over one block of Aida, using two strands of stranded cotton for full and half cross stitches. Work backstitches with one strand. When all stitching is complete, mount and frame your picture.

Oh, Christmas Tree

DMC stranded cotton

Full cross stitch (2 strands)

■ 312	597	＼ 838	＋ 3325	• blanc
▬ 321	− 598	∧ 839	3346	
‖ 334	666	840	／ 3347	E815 Light Effects
433	676	＼ 950	3348	
○ 435	U 677	3041	○ 3743	E3821 Light Effects
436	‖ 729	✕ 3042	3774	

Half cross stitch (2 strands)

334
3042
3325
／ blanc

Backstitch (1 strand)

— 413

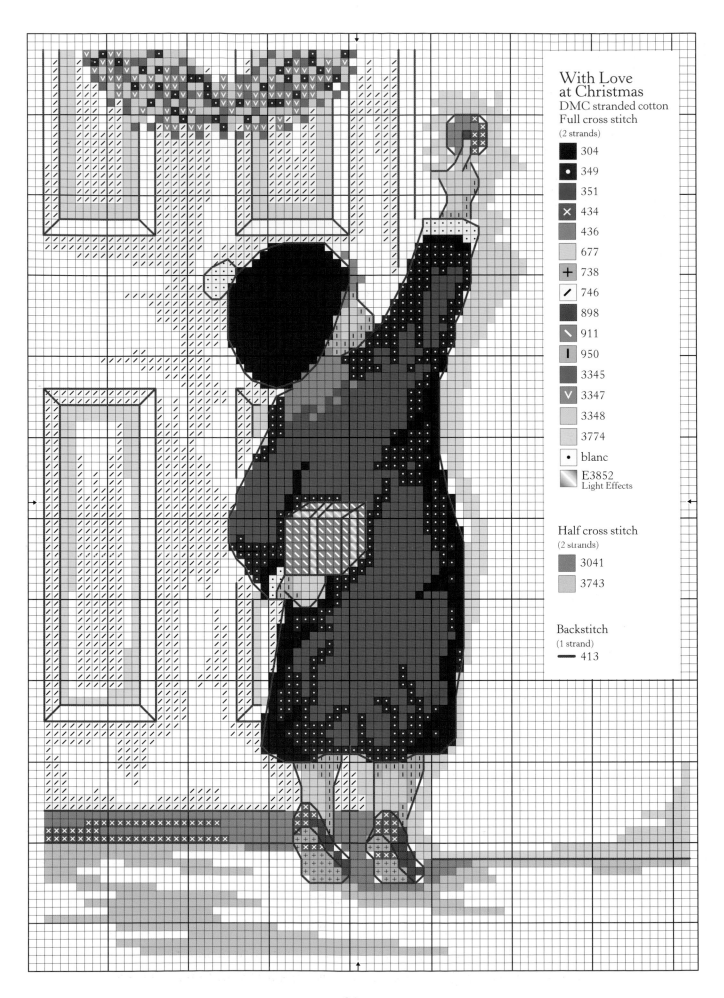

With Love
at Christmas
DMC stranded cotton
Full cross stitch
(2 strands)

■	304
⊡	349
■	351
✕	434
■	436
▨	677
+	738
╱	746
■	898
╲	911
I	950
■	3345
V	3347
▨	3348
▨	3774
•	blanc
◨	E3852 Light Effects

Half cross stitch
(2 strands)

■	3041
▨	3743

Backstitch
(1 strand)
—— 413

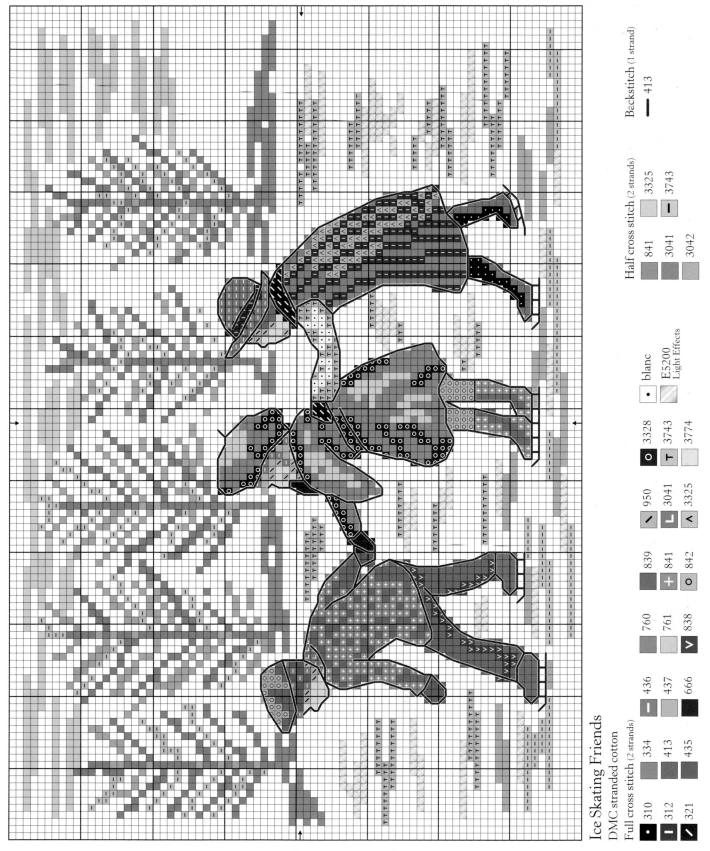

Ice Skating Friends

DMC stranded cotton

Full cross stitch (2 strands)

•	310		760		839	blanc
▬	334		761	+	841	o 3328
▬	413	✓	838	o 842	O 950
✓	435					
▬	436			/ 3041	3743
	437			L 3328	T 3743
▬	321			< 3325	■ 3774

Half cross stitch (2 strands)

	841	3325
	3041	I 3743
	3042	

Backstitch (1 strand)

— 413

Remember when. . .?

We looked forward to Christmas time as this meant snow might soon follow.
We would wake up to a magical white world and make a dash for the hills and
fields with make-shift toboggans, or sometimes just a tin tray to slide on.

87

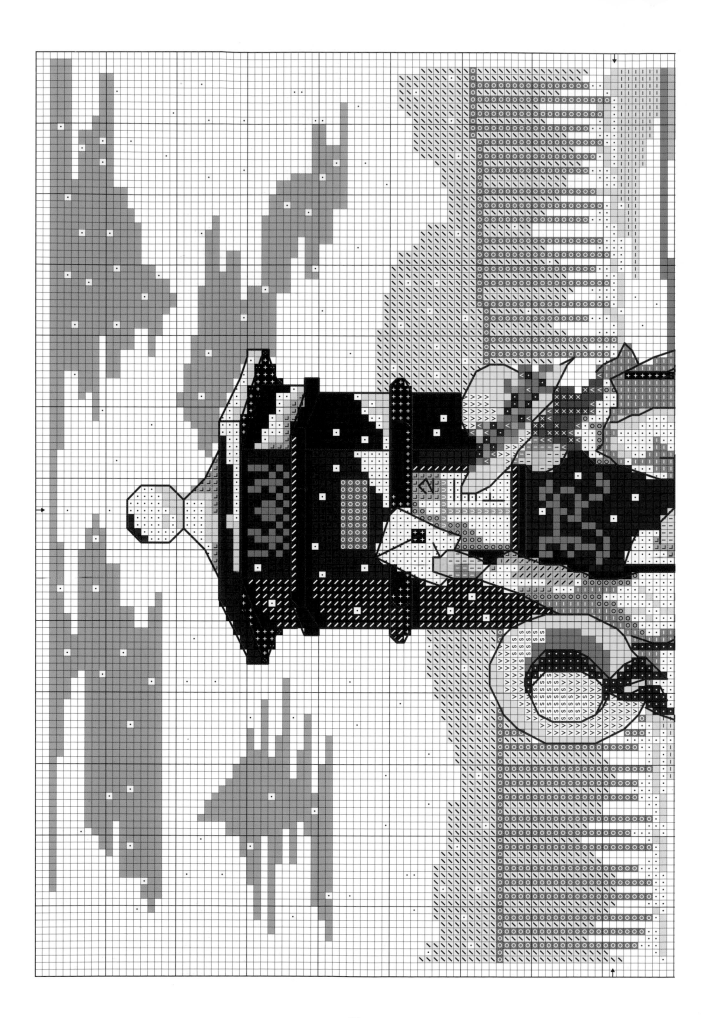

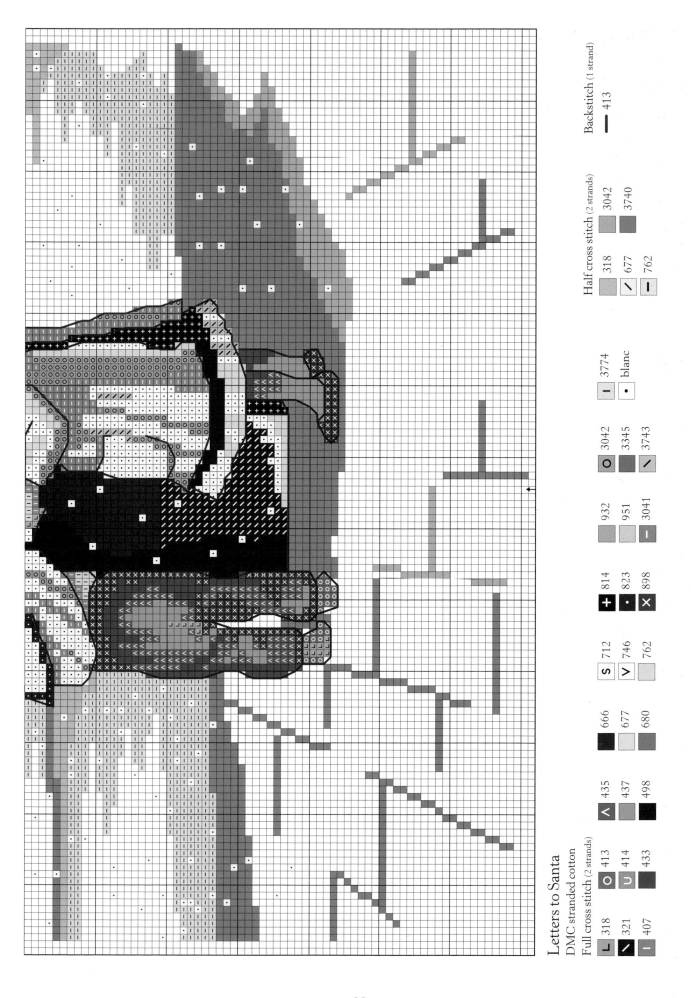

Letters to Santa

DMC stranded cotton

Full cross stitch (2 strands)

L	318	O	413		435		666	S	712	+	814	O	3042	I	3774
/	321	U	414	<	437		677	V	746	·	823		3345	·	blanc
I	407		433		498		680		762	X	898	/	3743		

Half cross stitch (2 strands)

	318		3042
/	677		3740
—	762		

Backstitch (1 strand)

— 413

THE FUN OF THE FAIR

As holiday resort towns developed in the early 20th century so too did the entertainments, the streets coming alive with musicians and actors, circus performers, minstrels, travelling photographers and peddlers, and Punch and Judy shows. While the middle and upper classes still preferred dignified activities, such as sedate

strolls along the promenade, those from the working classes escaping the city drudgery sought out noisier, more exciting entertainments, in particular fairs, circuses and pantomimes.

The steam-powered attractions of fairground rides were great favourites and 'white-knuckle' rides began to be built, such as the whirling Chair-o-Planes and the spinning Razzle Dazzle ride, 'The Grand Ariel Novelty'. In a kaleidoscope of colour, movement and sound, the Golden Gallopers – the carousel – also drew large crowds. The carousel was perhaps the most majestic of the fairground attractions, a brightly painted and lavishly gilded masterpiece of drama, romance and excitement.

The Carousel Horse

Experience all the fun of the fair on a wonderful carousel horse, rising, falling and circling in a whirl of colour to the sound of jolly organ music. (Stitching instructions, page 96.)

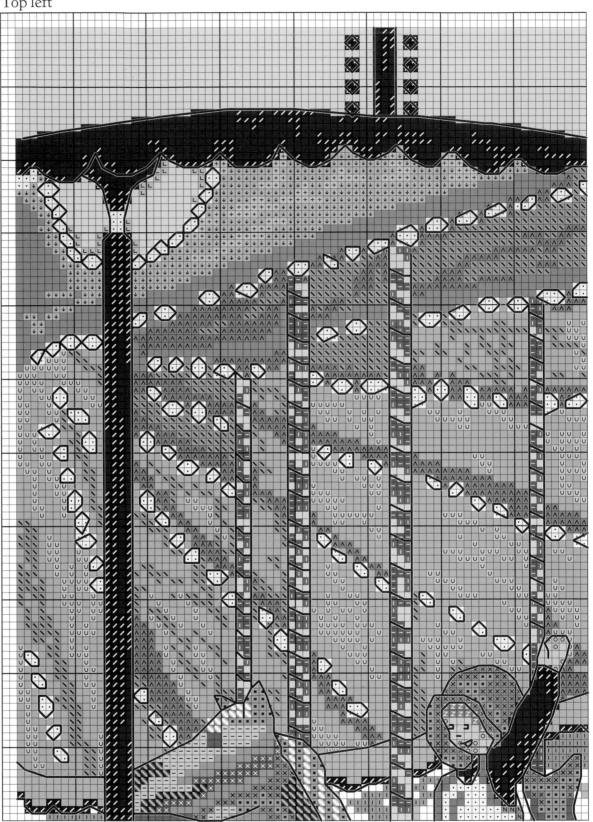

Carousel Horse
DMC stranded cotton
Full cross stitch (2 strands)

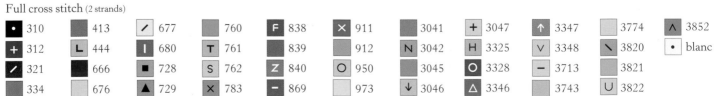

▪ 310	413	✓ 677	760	F 838	✗ 911	3041	+ 3047	↑ 3347	3774	∧ 3852
+ 312	L 444	I 680	T 761	839	912	N 3042	H 3325	V 3348	↘ 3820	• blanc
✗ 321	666	▪ 728	S 762	Z 840	O 950	3045	O 3328	– 3713	3821	
334	676	▲ 729	✗ 783	– 869	973	↓ 3046	△ 3346	3743	U 3822	

DMC Light Effects

Full cross stitch (2 strands)

- E815
- E825
- E3852

Half cross stitch (2 strands)

- 3325
- 3346
- 3347
- 3348
- 3755

Backstitch (1 strand)

- ▬ 413

Carousel Horse

DMC stranded cotton

Full cross stitch (2 strands)

• 310	413	✓ 677	760	F 838	✕ 911	3041	+ 3047	↑ 3347	3774	∧ 3852
+ 312	L 444	I 680	T 761	839	912	N 3042	H 3325	V 3348	✕ 3820	• blanc
✓ 321	666	■ 728	S 762	Z 840	O 950	3045	O 3328	− 3713	3821	
334	676	▲ 729	✕ 783	− 869	973	↓ 3046	△ 3346	3743	U 3822	

DMC Light Effects

Full cross stitch (2 strands)

- E815
- E825
- E3852

Half cross stitch (2 strands)

- 3325
- 3346
- 3347
- 3348
- 3755

Backstitch (1 strand)

— 413

The Carousel Horse

A century ago the merry-go-round or carousel was a favourite with all the family. The rides usually featured brightly painted horses but might also have chariots and even cockerels to ride on. Who could resist a ride on a magnificent prancing horse, frozen in mid-air gallop, mane and tail flying? This colourful design uses some DMC Light Effects threads to bring extra sparkle and glitter to the embroidery, echoing the gilding that was used on these rides.

THE CAROUSEL HORSE (PAGE 91)

Fabric
16-count ivory Aida (DMC DC88 712), 48 x 38cm (19 x 15in)

Threads
DMC stranded cotton (floss) as listed in the key – 1 skein of each colour and 2 skeins of 413, 973, 3316, 3347, 3348, 3821 and blanc; DMC Light Effects as listed in the key

Stitch Count
218h x 161w

Design Size
34.5 x 25.5cm (13¾ x 10in)

Stitches
Whole cross stitch, half cross stitch, backstitch

Stitch the Scene. . .
Prepare your fabric for work and mark the centre point (see page 98). Follow the chart on pages 92–95. Before beginning to stitch, you might find it easier to colour photocopy the chart and tape the four parts together. Work over one block of Aida, using two strands of stranded cotton for full and half cross stitches. Use two strands for Light Effects cross stitches (see page 99 for advice on using Light Effects threads). Work backstitches with one strand. When all stitching is complete, mount and frame your picture.

USE THE SCENE. . .

This design would also make an eye-catching and colourful scatter cushion for a child's room. You could stitch it on 14-count Aida to create a bigger finished design size, and then border the scene on all sides with a bright fabric before making up into a cushion.

Remember when. . .?

You could ride on a Golden Galloper or Whirlitzer for a only a penny, and the ride and the music of the organ seemed to go on forever.

Faye Whittaker

Alphabet Charts

You can use these alphabets and numbers to customize the designs in the book, for example, to add names and messages to greetings cards or to create a name plate for a door or journal cover. Plan the wording on graph paper before you start to stitch, to check the spacing looks balanced. The cross stitch and backstitch colours can easily be changed to suit the project.

Basic Materials and Techniques

The designs in this book are easy to stitch, requiring few materials and equipment and using only basic stitching techniques.

Fabrics

The designs have all been stitched over one block of a 16-count Aida fabric. You could use a 32-count evenweave if you prefer and stitch the designs over two threads. See page 103 for further information about DMC fabrics.

Threads

All of the designs have been worked with DMC stranded cotton (floss) and a few have used Light Effects threads for a metallic shine. Generally, use two strands for cross stitch and one strand for backstitch on 14- and 16-count Aida. See opposite for tips on working with Light Effects and page 103 for further information about DMC threads.

Equipment

A few basic tools are all you need to get started. See also page 104.

Needles

Use blunt tapestry needles for counted cross stitch. The commonest sizes used are 24 and 26 but the size depends on your project and personal preference. Avoid leaving a needle in the fabric unless it is gold plated or it may cause marks. If you plan to embellish your cross stitch with seed beads, use a beading needle (or fine 'sharp' needle), which is thinner.

Scissors

Use dressmaker's shears for cutting fabric and a small, sharp pair of pointed scissors for cutting embroidery threads.

Frames and Hoops

These are not essential, especially for small designs, but if you use one, choose one big enough to hold the complete design, to avoid marking fabric and flattening stitches.

Using Charts

❖ The designs are worked from colour charts with black or white symbols where necessary to identify colours more easily.

❖ Each square, both occupied and unoccupied, represents one block of Aida (or two threads of evenweave) unless stated otherwise.

❖ Each occupied square equals one cross stitch. Some charts use three-quarter cross stitches (sometimes referred to as fractional stitches) – these usually occupy half a square and are shown as a triangle.

❖ Half cross stitches (noted in the key) are used where the design needs to be less dense (often for backgrounds).

❖ French knots are shown on the charts by coloured circles (though in the chart on pages 38–39 the French knots are optional so are shown as cross stitch).

❖ Backstitch (and sometimes long stitch) is shown on charts by solid, coloured straight lines.

Calculating Design Size

Each project gives details of the stitch count and finished design size but if working the design on a different count fabric (to make the design larger or smaller), then you will need to be able to calculate the finished size.

❖ Count the number of stitches across the height of the design and then the width.

❖ Divide each of these numbers by the fabric count number, e.g., 160 stitches x 160 stitches ÷ by 16-count = a design size of 10 x 10in (25.4 x 25.4cm).

❖ Remember, working on evenweave usually means working over two threads not one block, so divide the fabric count by 2 before you start.

Preparing Fabric

❖ Press embroidery fabric if necessary before you begin stitching and trim the selvage or rough edges.

❖ Work from the middle of the piece of fabric and the middle of the chart wherever possible to ensure your design is centred on the fabric.

❖ Find the middle of the fabric by folding it in four and pressing lightly. Mark the folds with tailor's chalk or tacking (basting) following a fabric thread.

❖ When working with evenweave or linen, prepare as above but also sew a narrow hem around all raw edges to preserve the edges for finishing later.

Starting and Finishing Stitching

Unless indicated otherwise, begin stitching in the middle of a design to ensure an adequate margin for making up. If you start and finish stitching neatly and avoid knots your finished work will be smoother.

Knotless loop start

This start can be used with an *even* number of strands i.e., 2, 4 or 6. To stitch with two strands, begin with one strand about 80cm (30in). Double the thread and thread the needle with the two ends. Put the needle up through the fabric from the wrong side, where you intend to begin stitching, leaving the loop at the back. Form a half cross stitch, put the needle back through the fabric and through the waiting loop to anchor the stitch.

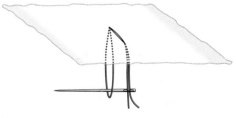

Knotless loop start

Away waste knot start

Start this way if using an *odd* number of strands. Thread your needle with the number of strands required and knot the end. Insert the needle into the right side of the fabric a little way away from where you wish to begin stitching. Work your stitching towards the knot and cut it off when the threads are anchored. The alternative is to snip off the knot, thread a needle and work under a few stitches to anchor it.

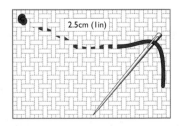

Away waste knot start

Finishing stitching

At the back of the work, pass the needle and thread under several stitches of the same or similar colour, and then snip off the loose end close to the stitching. You can begin a new colour in a similar way.

Working with Light Effects

Light Effects threads can be used on their own for maximum sparkle and shine or be mixed with other colours in the Light Effects range or with stranded cotton to create subtle effects.

When working with Light Effects threads, work with shorter lengths, about 30.5cm (12in), to reduce wear on the thread. These threads have a little more spring in them, so follow the threading diagram below, as this method holds the thread firmly in the needle. The same method can be used if working with two strands or two types of thread.

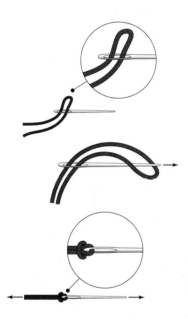

To thread Light Effects thread, form a loop of thread and thread the needle with the loop. Pass the loop over the point of the needle. Pull back so the loop tightens and fits snugly at the eye end of the needle

Working the Stitches

Backstitch

Backstitch is used for outlining a design or part of a design, to add detail or emphasis, or for lettering. It is added after the cross stitch has been completed, to prevent the backstitch line being broken by the cross stitches.

Follow the numbered sequence in the diagram, working over one block of Aida (or two threads of evenweave).

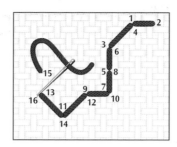

Working backstitch

Cross Stitch

This simple little stitch is the most commonly used stitch in this book. Cross stitches can be worked singly or in two journeys. For neat stitching, keep the top stitch facing the same direction.

Cross stitch on Aida To work a complete cross stitch, work over one block of Aida (or two threads of evenweave) and follow the numbered sequence in the diagram below: bring the needle up at 1, down at 2, up at 3 and down at 4. To work the adjacent stitch, bring the needle up at the bottom right-hand corner of the first stitch.

Working a single cross stitch on Aida

To work cross stitches in two journeys, work the first leg of the cross stitch as above but instead of completing the stitch, work the adjacent half stitch and continue on to the end of the row. Complete the crosses by working the other diagonals on the return journey.

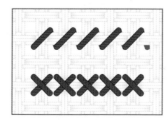

Working cross stitch in two journeys on Aida

Three-quarter Cross Stitch This is a fractional stitch that can produce the illusion of curves on cross stitch designs. It can be formed on either Aida or evenweave but is easier on evenweave.

Work the first half of a cross stitch as usual, i.e., a half cross stitch. Work the second 'quarter' stitch over the top and down into the central hole to anchor the first half of the stitch. If using Aida, you will need to push the needle through the centre of a block of the fabric. Where two three-quarter stitches lie back-to-back in the space of one full cross stitch, work both of the respective 'quarter' stitches into the central hole.

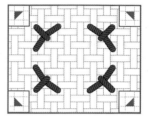

Working three-quarter cross stitch

Perfect Stitching

❖ Organize your threads before you start a project; using a thread organizer (see page 104) is a good idea as this will help to avoid confusion. Always include the thread manufacturer's name and shade number.

❖ Separate the strands on a skein of stranded cotton (floss), take the number you need, realign them and thread your needle.

❖ If using an embroidery hoop, make sure you use one big enough for the whole design and avoid placing it over worked stitches.

❖ Plan your route around a chart, counting over short distances to avoid mistakes.

❖ Where possible, work your cross stitch in two directions in a sewing movement – half cross stitch in one direction and then cover those original stitches with the second row. This forms single vertical lines on the back that are very neat and give somewhere to finish raw ends. For the neatest work, the top stitches should all face the same direction.

❖ If adding a backstitch outline, always add it after the cross stitch has been completed to prevent the solid line being broken.

FINISHING AND MAKING UP

This section gives advice on making up the designs into projects such as framed pictures, greetings cards and bookmarks. Some other ways to use the designs are suggested throughout the book. Refer to a DMC catalogue for other products.

Using Iron-On Interfacing

Your embroidery can be made much more adaptable if you back it with iron-on interfacing or adhesive; not only does this stabilize the stitches and prevent the fabric edges fraying but will allow you to apply your embroidery as a patch to ready-made items such as photograph albums. Follow the manufacturer's instructions for bonding the adhesive on to the back of the embroidery with a warm iron. If you want a frayed edge to the embroidery, cut a smaller piece of interfacing and fuse it centrally on the back of the stitching.

Adding a Patch to an Album

Many of the designs would look lovely displayed on the cover of a photograph album or a book. Back your embroidery with iron-on interfacing, as described above, allowing for a frayed edge all round if desired. Use craft glue to stick the embroidery to a piece of stiff card and then glue the card to the front of your album.

Mounting Work in Cards

Many of the smaller designs in the book or parts of the larger designs would make great greetings cards. There are many card blanks available from craft shops and mail-order suppliers and you can also make your own cards. The instructions opposite describe how to make a card with a window (aperture) – simply change the dimensions to suit the embroidery you wish to display.

Mounting Work on a Single-Fold Card

You can mount your embroidery on a single-fold card quite easily. Simply trim your embroidery to the size required, leaving two or three extra rows all round if you want a fringe. Pull away the outer fabric threads to form the fringe and use double-sided adhesive tape or craft glue to attach the embroidery to the front of your card. For a neat edge that does not fray, fuse iron-on adhesive to the back of your embroidery (see instructions, left) and then trim the embroidery to size before fixing it to the front of your card.

Making a Double-Fold Card with Aperture

1 Choose a card colour to complement your embroidery and cut a piece 30 x 12cm (12 x 4¾in) as shown in the diagram below. On the wrong side of the card, draw two lines dividing it into three sections of 10cm (4in). Score gently along each line with the back of a craft knife to make folding easier.

2 In the centre section, mark an aperture slightly bigger than the finished size of the design – the diagram shows an aperture of 5.7 x 5.7cm (2¼ x 2¼in), with a border of about 2.2cm (⅞in) along the top and sides. Cut out the aperture with a sharp craft knife, carefully cutting into the corners neatly. Trim the left edge of the first section by 2mm (⅛in) so that it lies flat when folded over to the inside of the card. This will cover the back of the stitching. Fold the left and then the right section on the scored lines.

Mounting Work into a Double-Fold Card

1 Lay the card right side up on top of the design so the stitching is in the middle of the aperture. Place a pin in each corner and remove the card. Trim the fabric to within about 1.5cm (⅝in) so it fits into the card.

2 On the wrong side of the card, stick double-sided tape around the aperture and peel off the backing tape (some ready-made cards already have this tape in place). Place the card over the design, using the pins to guide it into position. Press down firmly so the fabric is stuck securely to the card. Remove the pins.

3 On the wrong side of the card, stick more tape around the edge of the middle section. Peel off the backing tape, fold the left section in to cover the back of the stitching, pressing down firmly.

Making a double-fold aperture card

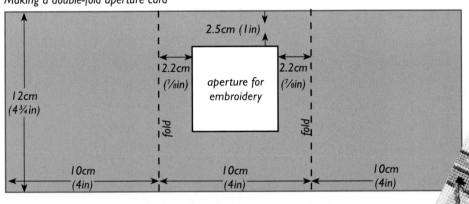

Making Up a Bookmark

Smaller designs or sections from some of the larger designs would make perfect bookmarks. Stitch the design on to a piece of Aida or evenweave and turn the edges to the back in a narrow hem along the top and sides. Fold the bottom of the fabric piece to form a point and slipstitch in place and then add a tassel to finish (see instructions overleaf). For an even quicker bookmark use an Aida or linen band, which come in varying widths and have decorative side edges that do not require hemming.

Mounting and Framing a Picture

Many of the cross stitch embroideries in this book have been designed to make stunning pictures. You could take your work to a professional framer who will help you chose a suitable mount and frame for the design. Alternatively, you could mount the work yourself, using the following instructions and a ready-made frame. You will need: a suitable picture frame; mount board the same size as the frame; wadding (batting); double-sided adhesive tape; pins and crochet cotton or strong thread.

1 Cut your mount board to the size of the picture frame aperture (draw around the sheet of glass). Cut a piece of wadding (batting) the same size and secure it to the mount board with double-sided tape. Lay your embroidery face up on the wadding (batting) and when you are happy with the position, push a line of pins down each side into the board. Check the stitching is straight, and trim the fabric to leave about 5cm (2in) all round.

2 Fold the excess fabric to the back. Thread a needle with a long length of crochet cotton or strong thread, knot the end and lace the two opposite sides together on the back, starting at one end and working in a zigzag manner. When you reach the other end, pull the lacing tight and adjust the laced threads one by one before

finishing off. Repeat this process on the two remaining edges. Alternatively, you could use double-sided tape to secure the fabric to the back of the board.

3 Fold down the corners and stitch neatly into place. Remove the pins and assemble your work in its frame. It is not necessary to use the glass; this often flattens the stitches when they are pushed against it.

Making a Tassel

A tassel makes a nice finishing touch, for example at the end of a bookmark or on the corners of a cushion or scented sachet.

1 Cut a rectangular piece of stiff card, about 1.5cm (½in) longer than the desired size of the tassel. Choose a thread colour to match your project and wrap the thread around the card to the desired thickness.

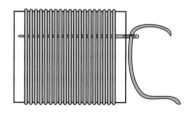

2 Slip a length of thread through the top of the tassel and tie in a knot. Cut the threads at the bottom of the tassel and then slide the threads off the card. Bind the top third of the tassel with another length of thread and then trim all the tassel ends to the same length

DMC Fabrics, Threads and Kits

DMC Fabrics

There are various types of fabric available for cross stitch and other forms of embroidery and some of the most popular are described here.

DMC Aida

Aida fabrics are usually made from cotton and are woven with the threads grouped in bundles to form a square pattern on the fabric. Aida is easy to work from, especially for beginners. It is available in pre-cut shapes and by the metre in a wide range of colours and in various counts – 6, 11, 14, 16 and 18. The 'count' or gauge of a fabric determines how many stitches can be worked per inch (2.5cm), so the higher the count, the more stitches to the inch.

DMC Evenweave

Evenweave fabrics are made of cotton and various fibres and are woven with single threads. As with Aida, these fabrics are available in a wide range of colours, in pre-cut pieces or by the metre. Cross stitch is normally worked over two threads of evenweave and the counts available are 22, 25, 27 and 28.

DMC Linen

This fabric is made from 100% linen, is woven from single threads and, like evenweave, is normally worked over two fabric threads. It is available in various colours, in 12, 25, 28 and 32 counts.

DMC Aida and Evenweave Bands

Bands are very useful as trims, to personalize accessories and for quick-stitch projects. They are available in various widths, colours and counts and with different decorative edgings.

DMC Threads

Many different types of threads are available from DMC. The designs in this book use stranded cottons and some Light Effects threads but why not try some of the others in their range?

DMC Stranded Cotton (floss)

This six-stranded divisible thread is perfect for stitching on all types of fabric and is available in a choice of 465 colourfast colours. It is double mercerized to give it an attractive gloss comparable to silk.

DMC Linen Threads

This six-stranded divisible thread has all the benefits of stranded cotton but is made from the 100% linen fibres to bring a matt and natural-looking appearance to stitching. It is available in 24 natural colours and is perfect for cross stitch, embroidery and Hardanger work.

DMC Light Effects Threads

These six-stranded divisible speciality threads are available in 36 glistening colours to add light and reflective qualities to needlework projects. There are six different thread 'families' – gold and silver, precious stones, antique gilt finishes, precious metal effects, pearlescent effects and fluorescent effects. Colour codes for these threads begin with E. See page 99 for tips on working with these threads.

DMC Accessories

There are many accessories available to make cross stitch and other forms of embroidery easier and more pleasurable and DMC have a wide range of useful items, a few of which are shown here.

DMC Kits

Most of the designs in this book are adapted from existing DMC All Our Yesterdays kits. The range of kits changes a little from year to year and

new designs are always being added, so refer to an up-to-date DMC catalogue to see all the designs that are currently available. Two of the kits are shown here. Your local needlecraft store or retailer should have a catalogue or information on obtaining one. In the catalogue you will also find a wealth of other cross stitch designs in kit form, suitable for all skill levels, from complete beginner to experienced stitchers.

A kit has everything you need to create beautiful cross stitch projects, including needle, fabric, threads, chart and any accessories the design requires. All kits have clear instructions and easy-to-follow diagrams.

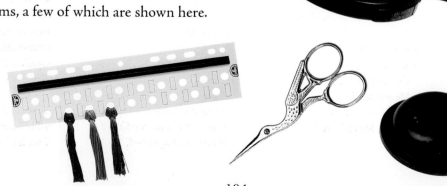

SUPPLIERS

UK
DMC Creative World Ltd
Pullman Road,
Wigston,
Leicestershire LE18 2DY
tel: (44) 116-2 81 10 40
www.dmccreative.co.uk
www.dmc.com

USA
The DMC Corporation
South Hackensack Avenue
Port Kearny Building ~10F
South Kearny
NJ 07032
tel: 1-973-589 0606
www.dmc-usa.com

FRANCE
DMC
5 Avenue de Suisse
BP 89
68314 Illzach Cedex
tel: (33) 03.89.31.91.89

INDEX